CW01260819

A Word From
Kevin Douglas Keenan
Akin Gump

I am pleased to be a part of this important new book, *Inside the Minds: Energy Law Settlements and Negotiations*, by Aspatore Books. As a partner in one of the world's largest law firms, I am but a small part of an institution that got its start in energy and is today involved in energy-related transactions and dispute resolution around the world. Since the firm's early days in the 1940s, Akin Gump has been a key advisor to the oil and gas industry. Originally, our involvement was purely domestic. With the opening of Akin Gump's Moscow and London offices in 1994 and 1997, respectively, and with the addition of offices in Taipei and Dubai in 2005 and Beijing in 2007, our reach is now truly global. Because energy is the lifeblood of the world's economy, and because managing the flow of energy is crucial to sustaining a healthy and dynamic global marketplace, Akin Gump's well-established position as a leader in the provision of energy-related legal advice offers me a solid platform to engage in an area of practice that I thoroughly enjoy and that actually makes a difference in the world at large. It is my hope that you will enjoy reading this book as much as I enjoyed contributing to it.

AKIN GUMP STRAUSS HAUER & FELD LLP

Recognized for its multidisciplinary capabilities and its team of outstanding professionals, Akin Gump Strauss Hauer & Feld LLP is a leading international law firm dedicated to providing innovative legal services to individuals and institutions. Founded in 1945, the firm has become one of the largest in the world, with over 900 lawyers representing regional, national and international clients in more than 50 practice areas. Today, Akin Gump's lawyers are found in Austin, Dallas, Dubai, Houston, London, Los Angeles, Moscow, New York, Philadelphia, San Antonio, San Francisco, Silicon Valley, Taipei and Washington, D.C. In early 2007, Akin Gump will open its newest office in Beijing.

Akin Gump's energy lawyers have advised on projects and transactions around the world, from the purchase of oil & gas interests in Egypt to the sale of natural gas in Vietnam. From the $21.3 billion acquisition of Kerr-McGee and Western Gas Resources by Anadarko Petroleum to the largest private maritime fleet acquisition in history for various Qatari joint ventures among Qatar Petroleum, ExxonMobil, Shell and ConocoPhillips, Akin Gump lawyers are trusted advisors to some of the world's largest companies and projects. For more information, please visit us at www.akingump.com.

AKIN GUMP
STRAUSS HAUER & FELD LLP
Attorneys at Law

Praise for *Inside the Minds*

"Need-to-read inside information and analysis that will improve your bottom line—the best source in the business." – Daniel J. Moore, Member, Harris Beach LLP

"The *Inside the Minds* series is a valuable probe into the thoughts, perspectives, and techniques of accomplished professionals…" – Chuck Birenbaum, Partner, Thelen Reid & Priest

"Aspatore has tapped into a goldmine of knowledge and expertise ignored by other publishing houses." – Jack Barsky, Managing Director, Information Technology and CIO, ConEdison Solutions

"Unlike any other publisher—actual authors that are on the front lines of what is happening in industry." – Paul A. Sellers, Executive Director, National Sales, Fleet and Remarketing, Hyundai Motor America

"A snapshot of everything you need..." – Charles Koob, Co-Head of Litigation Department, Simpson Thacher & Bartlet

"Everything good books should be—honest, informative, inspiring, and incredibly well written." – Patti D. Hill, President, BlabberMouth PR

"Great information for both novices and experts." – Patrick Ennis, Partner, ARCH Venture Partners

"A rare peek behind the curtains and into the minds of the industry's best." – Brandon Baum, Partner, Cooley Godward

"Intensely personal, practical advice from seasoned deal-makers." – Mary Ann Jorgenson, Coordinator of Business Practice Area, Squire, Sanders & Dempsey

"Great practical advice and thoughtful insights." – Mark Gruhin, Partner, Schmeltzer, Aptaker & Shepard PC

"Reading about real-world strategies from real working people beats the typical business book hands down." – Andrew Ceccon, CMO, OnlineBenefits Inc.

"Books of this publisher are syntheses of actual experiences of real-life, hands-on, front-line leaders—no academic or theoretical nonsense here. Comprehensive, tightly organized, yet nonetheless motivational!" – Lac V. Tran, Senior Vice President, CIO, and Associate Dean, Rush University Medical Center

"Aspatore is unlike other publishers…books feature cutting-edge information provided by top executives working on the front lines of an industry." – Debra Reisenthel, President and CEO, Novasys Medical Inc.

To my loving wife, Jill, and our four beautiful children – Savannah, Madison, Sydney and Wyatt. While they care little for the nuances of energy law (as long as there's gas at the pump), their patience for my expenditure of time on the road is limitless. And I am grateful.

INSIDE THE MINDS

Energy Law Settlements and Negotiations

Leading Lawyers on Dealing with Regulatory Commissions, Understanding Political and Market Forces, and Making the Right Deal

ASPATORE BOOKS
C-LEVEL BUSINESS INTELLIGENCE

BOOK IDEA SUBMISSIONS

If you are a C-Level executive or senior lawyer interested in submitting a book idea or manuscript to the Aspatore editorial board, please e-mail authors@aspatore.com. Aspatore is especially looking for highly specific book ideas that would have a direct financial impact on behalf of a reader. Completed books can range from 20 to 2,000 pages—the topic and "need to read" aspect of the material are most important, not the length. Include your book idea, biography, and any additional pertinent information.

ARTICLE SUBMISSIONS

If you are a C-Level executive or senior lawyer interested in submitting an article idea (or content from an article previously written but never formally published), please e-mail authors@aspatore.com. Aspatore is especially looking for highly specific articles that would be part of our *Executive Reports* series. Completed reports can range from 2 to 20 pages and are distributed as coil-bound reports to bookstores nationwide. Include your article idea, biography, and any additional information.

GIVE A VIDEO LEADERSHIP SEMINAR

If you are interested in giving a Video Leadership Seminar™, please e-mail the ReedLogic speaker board (a partner of Aspatore Books) at speakers@reedlogic.com. If selected, ReedLogic would work with you to identify the topic, create interview questions, and coordinate the filming of the interview. ReedLogic studios then professionally produce the video and turn it into a Video Leadership Seminar™ on your area of expertise. The final product is burned onto DVD and distributed to bookstores nationwide.

Published by Aspatore Inc.

For corrections, company/title updates, comments, or any other inquiries, please e-mail store@aspatore.com.

First Printing, 2006
10 9 8 7 6 5 4 3 2 1

Copyright © 2006 by Aspatore Inc. All rights reserved. Printed in the United States of America. No part of this publication may be reproduced or distributed in any form or by any means, or stored in a database or retrieval system, except as permitted under Sections 107 or 108 of the U.S. Copyright Act, without prior written permission of the publisher. This book is printed on acid-free paper.

ISBN 1-59622-510-6
Library of Congress Control Number: 2006933437

Inside the Minds project manager, Carey Fries; edited by Eddie Fournier

Material in this book is for educational purposes only. This book is sold with the understanding that neither any of the authors nor the publisher are engaged in rendering legal, accounting, investment, or any other professional service. Neither the publisher nor the authors assume any liability for any errors or omissions, or for how this book or its contents are used or interpreted, or for any consequences resulting directly or indirectly from the use of this book. For legal advice or any other, please consult your personal lawyer or the appropriate professional.

The views expressed by the individuals in this book (or the individuals on the cover) do not necessarily reflect the views shared by the companies they are employed by (or the companies mentioned in this book). The employment status and affiliations of authors with the companies referenced are subject to change.

Energy Law Settlements and Negotiations

Leading Lawyers on Dealing with Regulatory Commissions, Understanding Political and Market Forces, and Making the Right Deal

CONTENTS

Kevin D. Keenan 13
GOING GLOBAL: CHALLENGES AND OPPORTUNITIES FOR ENERGY LAWYERS

James M. Avery 37
ENERGY LAW: PEELING BACK THE LAYERS

Chad Mills 45
PREPARING FOR AND SUCCEEDING IN NEGOTIATIONS

Sara Schotland 53
WINNING STRATEGIES BEFORE THE FERC

Philip L. Comella 65
GLOBAL WARMING AND THE COMING REGULATION OF CO_2 EMISSIONS

Daniel Yost, Lou Soto, and Mitch Zuklie 79
PRACTICING CLEAN ENERGY LAW: A FOCUS ON SOLAR

Charles E. Frost Jr.   89
PROTECTING AN ENERGY COMPANY'S
INTELLECTUAL PROPERTY

Edward G. Kehoe   101
PERFORMING AN EFFECTIVE
COST/BENEFIT ANALYSIS

Frank A. Caro Jr.   109
GETTING TO KNOW THE CLIENT

Todd Culwell   117
BRINGING THE DEAL TO CLOSURE:
THE ULTIMATE GOAL

Jeffrey D. Komarow   129
ENERGY REGULATION AND POLICY
IN A TIME OF CHANGE: A MODEST
AGENDA FOR UTILITY REGULATORS,
AN AMBITIOUS AGENDA FOR FEDERAL
POLICYMAKERS

Appendices   143

Going Global: Challenges and Opportunities for Energy Lawyers

Kevin D. Keenan

Partner

Akin Gump Strauss Hauer & Feld LLP

Energy is the lifeblood of the world's economy, and managing the flow of energy is crucial to sustaining a healthy and dynamic global marketplace. As a vital part of all energy transactions, energy lawyers play a significant role not only in the financial and legal well-being of their clients, but also in the larger sphere of domestic and international energy trade. Simply put, energy law is not a field for those with little interest in what transpires beyond their own municipality, state, province, or nation; it is an area of law that demands knowledge of and engagement with the global community.

Putting aside for the moment the recent surge in energy prices, which has made a number of previously risky projects much less so as commodity prices far outstrip baseline assumptions underlying project economics, the overall risk profile for most energy companies is on the rise as hydrocarbons are increasingly located in remote areas onshore and offshore or in difficult terrains such as the frozen tundra of the far north. The significant time and volume of investment dollars, despite enhanced recovery techniques, has made mitigation of risk an enterprise-wide strategic mandate at leading companies. As a result, legal matters figure prominently into a client's overall risk profile. In addition, the cost of building special-purpose tankers, oil, gas, and products pipelines, infrastructure required for liquefied natural gas (LNG), liquefied petroleum gas (LPG) and gas-to-liquids (GTL) projects, as well as traditional crude oil refining facilities are on the rise. Furthermore, all of these types of investments are subject to increasingly stringent regulatory scrutiny. Thus, the universe of risks that management teams face at energy companies engaged in these types of projects is rapidly expanding and the need for sound legal advice and aggressive mitigation strategies is more acute than ever before.

My own practice involves negotiating terms and conditions related to the sale and transportation of oil, natural gas, oil products, coal, and petrochemicals. Very often, this involves moving such products across international borders, either on land or by sea. Because energy is rarely found close to the markets that demand it, there is a constant need to transport energy from source to market. Whether the energy being moved is coal, crude oil, crude oil products (e.g., diesel fuel, gasoline, etc.), LNG, LPG, or various petrochemicals derived from crude oil or natural gas, complicated transportation contracts are often called for to get such energy from source to market. Some of the energy used in homes and businesses today reaches the market via pipelines, while some of it reaches the market via marine transportation. In either case, there are risks and costs to be minimized and mitigated during the journey. Depending on which side of the transaction I represent, I look for different ways to accomplish that goal for my client.

I also help clients develop oil and gas discoveries in various parts of the world, purchase and sell interests in such discoveries and, from time to time, develop infrastructure to refine and/or distribute such discoveries. At the heart of every such transaction are a multitude of contracts that allocate risks and rewards among the parties. I advise on the strengths and weaknesses of those contracts and attempt, for my clients, to improve their positions *vis-à-vis* their counterparties or partners. While it is not my job in this context to decide whether my client should shoulder a particular risk or negotiate contractual language to mitigate it, it is my job to identify that risk and fully apprise my client of the potential ramifications arising from it.

Components of Energy Law

Oil and gas law is inextricably bound up with questions of land use and property rights. To put it simply, oil and gas law has traditionally been about the dirt and who has the right to be on it and drill into it. This involves issues such as the terms and conditions under which an oil and gas prospector is entitled to remain on the land while drilling for oil. If your lawyer is not in tune with standard practice, you may find yourself having signed away a lease that doesn't hold the oil prospector to any timeframe at all and, in essence, locks up your land indefinitely regardless of whether a discovery is made. The worst case scenario, in this regard, is for you to own land under which there are known deposits of oil and/or gas and lease it to someone for an indefinite period without any ability to terminate the lease for lack of effort. Meanwhile, your neighbor, who sits atop the same deposits (the laws of physics, it seems, do not respect property lines on the surface), leases to a competent prospector who drills, discovers oil and/or gas, and then proceeds—legally, in the U.S. and other jurisdictions, under the rule of capture—to drain the entire deposit. While the above is clearly an oversimplification, it is the competent oil and gas lawyer who knows his or her way around the standard lease and can, depending on which side of the transaction he or she is engaged, protect the driller, as lessee, or the landowner, as lessor, under the terms and conditions of a market-based oil and gas lease.

Oil and gas law has evolved over time, however, as arrangements in addition to the standard oil and gas lease have become necessary. Today's energy lawyer may spend his or her entire career working on commercial transactions involving oil and/or gas and may never negotiate an oil and gas lease *per se*. Such commercial transactions may include pipeline transportation agreements, tolling agreements, gas sale and purchase agreements, crude oil purchase agreements, time or voyage charters in respect of oil, petrochemical, LNG or LPG tankers, shipbuilding contracts for oil, petrochemical, LNG or LPG tankers, etc. As the world becomes smaller and smaller with the advent of new technologies, new trends in moving goods from place to place, new international conventions and cross-border legal regimes, evolving regulatory schemes and extraterritorial applications of domestic laws, the range of knowledge an energy lawyer must consider is expanding rapidly.

While the areas involving energy law are very much interconnected, if I had to break energy law down into separate components, I would do so along long-discussed industry lines as follows:

Upstream

This business segment includes the traditional oil and gas law described above. It also includes dealing with host governments in obtaining concessions to drill for what are, in most jurisdictions outside the United States, state-owned resources. Unlike the United States, very few jurisdictions permit private citizens to hold title to mineral rights, most such rights being owned by the government under whose land the resource is found. In order to develop these resources, the common approach is to enter into what are typically called production sharing contracts, concession agreements, or similar documents under which a prospector will be given the right to conduct seismic surveys of a given piece of land (or seabed, if offshore). Typically, the prospector will commit to spending a minimum amount of money in conducting prospecting operations and drilling a minimum number of prospecting wells within a specified period of time. If the prospector makes a discovery, he or she will be entitled to a certain amount for cost recovery and, thereafter, a percentage of what he or she finds, with the government being entitled to the remainder, paid either "in kind" or in hard currency, depending on the host country's needs and preferences. Upstream work in today's energy marketplace typically involves a significant amount of international exposure and negotiation with foreign governments given the locations throughout the world where energy is being found.

Hydrocarbon exploration and production is a capital-intensive, long-term business proposition. As a function of geopolitical risks, global environmental and sustainable development concerns, and supply and demand imbalances, companies operating in this sector are managing heightened risks, negotiating with varied cultures and government structures, and spreading and mitigating financial and operational risks through innovative business structures. Energy lawyers must draft agreements with business partners, financial institutions, and sovereign states that take a heightened risk universe into account and position their clients for success as best they can under ever-changing circumstances. As easily accessible hydrocarbon deposits diminish, exploration and production projects have become longer-term and more expensive in nature. As a result, the risk of failure or significant delay is heightened. The importance of research and development in the energy sector is on the rise again and energy lawyers must be familiar with a wider variety of techniques used in oil sands, coal bed methane, gas-to-liquids and liquefied natural gas, as well as a widening array of equipment.

Midstream

The midstream segment typically includes transportation of hydrocarbons from their source to market. Participants in the midstream market may include public or private operators of oil and natural gas pipelines, shipbuilders and various owners and operators of oil, LNG, LPG and various crude oil product and petrochemical tankers. A number of specialty businesses operate in the midstream sector, including fuel wholesalers and distributors and energy trading operations.

Much midstream legal work involves assisting clients with compliance matters related to the environmental, health and safety issues intrinsic in hydrocarbon processing, as well as cross-border issues related to overlapping international, regional, national, and local regulation and administrative practices. Oil must be transported via pipeline or tanker; natural gas must be transported via pipeline or LNG tanker. I spend a considerable amount of time in the midstream arena assisting clients with maritime transportation of hydrocarbons. Contracts between suppliers of crude oil or natural gas and commercial end users, such as refiners or power plant operators, are complex in nature, as there are a number of risks on both sides of such transactions to be addressed that include pricing, timing, conditions of delivery and resolution of disputes when unexpected events occur such as delays or accidents related to weather or human error.

As the energy industry continues to consolidate in response to scarce supply, the midstream segment has undergone considerable change in mature markets. Regional consolidation in Europe, significant disposition of assets in the United States, as well as negotiation and planning for massive pipeline projects to connect the frontier to mature markets, are examples of key changes underway. As a result of these activities and what I would call a baseload of traditional midstream work surrounding existing energy projects and infrastructure, transactional lawyers have been heavily involved in the midstream segment of the energy business in recent years.

Downstream

This business segment typically includes refining of crude oil, natural gas, and petrochemicals and the marketing of such hydrocarbons to end users. This end of the energy value chain is usually closest to markets where demand for energy is significant. Reliable and affordable energy is an implicit expectation of energy consumers that must be addressed by refiners and marketers. In addition, as refineries and petrochemical plants are most often located close to their intended market (i.e., major population centers), there is, as a rule, heightened sensitivity to environmental, health, and safety issues, especially in more developed economies.

Legal matters in the downstream sector parallel those in the midstream sector significantly. Legal work for downstream clients can span a number of areas of legal specialization including contracts between refiners and marketers (including retailers such as convenience store chains and service station franchisees), environmental, health and safety measures related to responsible plant operation, even labor and employment matters related to plant and retail operations.

Crossover Points

In many ways, energy law is no different than any other area of the law. To be effective, a lawyer must know the law and be able to communicate how the law applies to the facts at issue. Below are three areas, among many, where I believe energy law enjoys common ground with other areas of practice.

Staying Current on Shifting Ground

As in many other areas of law, energy law is forever changing. If oil and gas law has traditionally been "about the dirt," that dirt is constantly shifting underfoot—in some cases quite literally, as illustrated below in the discussion of WLNG's failure to obtain siting approval due to the presence of fault lines at its preferred location. In most cases, however, that shifting entails ever-changing laws and regulations. The challenge for the energy lawyer, particularly the energy lawyer involved in domestic and international projects, is to stay abreast of the current state of the law and the countless regulations implementing such laws.

On the domestic front, changing oil, gas and power regulations is a reality with which energy lawyers must be ever cognizant. In recent years, due to events with which most are well aware, the United States has enacted new laws and changed existing laws to, among other things, (i) provide incentives for increased domestic oil and gas exploration and production, (ii) mandate the stockpiling of crude oil and heating oil in the Strategic Petroleum Reserve, the Naval Petroleum Reserve and the Northeast Home Heating Oil Reserve, (iii) extend the Federal Energy Regulatory Commission's exclusive jurisdiction to include the siting, construction, operation, and expansion of onshore LNG terminals, (iv) provide mandates and incentives for the use of dual-fueled vehicles, the production of alternative fuels and the phasing out of certain fuel additives such as methyl tertiary butyl ether (MTBE, as it is commonly known), and (v) promote the development of and investment in advanced electricity transmission technologies and production infrastructure.

Internationally, the same trend is found. A number of countries within the European Union are grappling with security concerns over long-term gas supply. These concerns were exacerbated last winter when Russia flexed newly found economic muscle and curtailed gas supplies to the Ukraine. As a result, LNG continues to be a hot topic in Europe—increasingly so in Eastern Europe and the Baltic States of Latvia, Lithuania and Estonia, all of which have traditionally been dependent upon Russian gas. As a result, it is highly likely over the next few years that regulatory changes will be made and laws enacted to relax the development burden normally associated with siting, constructing and operating new LNG import terminals.

In the developing world, countries in producing regions are constantly updating their regulatory frameworks to ensure that they get what they consider to be a fair share of the resources being taken out of the ground. Some of these changes are minor in scope and effect; others are more fundamental and far-reaching. For example, in 2002, Nigeria's parliament approved changes to an oil revenue-sharing law that gives state governments a share of revenues from offshore oil and gas. State governors in Nigeria had warned that the troubled Niger Delta would eventually erupt in violence if the federal government did not amend a law that gave it full claim to offshore reserves and shut states out completely. To illustrate a more fundamental shift in legal regimes governing oil and gas, multinationals involved in exploration and production activities in Venezuela and Bolivia have in recent times seen their investments jeopardized by changing political tides. In Bolivia, President Evo Morales signed a decree in May of 2006 stating that all hydrocarbon reserves were to be nationalized. Venezuela, under populist President Hugo Chavez, recently voided drilling contracts with multinational companies at more than thirty of the country's most prolific oil fields, demanding new contracts that give Petróleos de Venezuela SA, the state oil company, a 60 percent stake in production. And Ecuador is said to be finalizing a law that could limit "excessive" profits by foreign crude producers.

Clearly, the shifting ground of regulatory and legal regimes can be a challenge for the international energy lawyer as he or she seeks to mitigate the risks involved in doing business in these jurisdictions. Obviously, one cannot hope to be able to mitigate a risk unless one is aware of it. Staying abreast of geopolitical developments and trends, as well as the means by which associated risks can be ameliorated contractually, is also of paramount importance to the effective energy lawyer.

The Power of Words

Contracts, whether in the energy sector or elsewhere, are built with words, and words have a great deal of power. Consider the ramifications, for example, of adding the word "not" in a strategic place in a contract. Three simple letters, when incorrectly placed in a binding contract, can mean millions or even billions of dollars of exposure. Of course, the above example is not difficult to appreciate—hyperbole to make my point—but it demonstrates the necessity of a contract lawyer who is detail-oriented and has a talent for weeding out or modifying ambiguous or potentially troublesome language in a contract. As these documents can often run to hundreds of pages, a sharp eye is truly as valuable as a sharp tongue or sharp pencil. A mentor of mine once said, "As lawyers, we don't make widgets. We write and we advocate." Left unsaid, but clearly implied, was the message that one must appreciate and master the power of words to succeed in this business.

The danger of ambiguous language in a document is the potential it brings for future litigation. It is the transactional lawyer's job, first and foremost, to keep his or her client out of litigation or arbitration by drafting the contract in such a way as to avoid any dispute as to what was intended. It would be inaccurate to say that ambiguity is no one's friend—it is, after all, ambiguous and poorly drafted contracts that keep commercial litigators happy, well paid and busy—but it certainly does nothing to benefit the parties to the transaction itself. Many of the disputes that arise over contracts of any type could be avoided with more careful attention to linguistic clarity.

Beyond the drafting and oversight of contract negotiations, the value of a good lawyer and business advisor resides in the ability to see a situation objectively, consider the universe of risks a venture may face, and build effective mitigation of those potential risks into the legal agreements drafted on behalf of the client. Only the client can determine the risks to be taken, but executives look to their legal advisors to identify and mitigate risk whenever possible.

The Importance of Inquiry

Effective lawyers—all effective lawyers—ask good questions. Effective lawyers ask a lot of questions. One cannot hope to understand the context in which a deal is being negotiated unless one asks the right questions. One cannot hope to craft, in cooperation with the client, an effective strategy for implementing a project, consummating an acquisition, or prosecuting a case without exhaustive inquiry. For example, suppose a client comes to you and engages you to represent them in starting up an exploration and production operation in a foreign jurisdiction. The prudent lawyer, practicing energy law or otherwise, would want to know the answers to a number of questions before ever beginning to form a strategy for the client.

To list but a few of these questions, consider the following: Are there any restrictions on foreign participation in exploration and production? Are there requirements of governmental or private local participation in the enterprise? Are there limitations on percentage of foreign ownership? Does the projected enterprise require formal governmental approval in advance or some form of license? If so, what governmental agency receives and/or approves the application? What information is required to be furnished? What fees are required to be paid in connection with the application? What restrictions are there on the use or exploitation of natural resources? Must a concession agreement or production sharing contract be obtained in order to exploit natural resources? If so, for what period and under what conditions? What types of restrictions will be imposed on the use or disposition of assets covered by the concession? What legal protection do industrial property rights such as patents, models, designs, trademarks and trade names receive, and is there discrimination between those developed locally and abroad? Are there any restrictions on repatriation of investments and remission of earnings? Is local currency freely convertible to U.S. dollars or another common currency? How do foreign exchange regulations affect repatriation of cash investments, investments in tangible goods and investments in intangibles?

The above-listed questions merely scratch the surface. One would also need to consider (i) the type of entity to be formed to undertake the foreign exploration and production activities and hold the exploration and production assets, (ii) the manner in which business should be conducted in the foreign jurisdiction (e.g., are audits required, what types of records must be kept, what type of financial reports must be submitted and with what frequency, etc.), (iii) whether there are any foreign investment incentives available under the circumstances, (iv) what tax treatment the exploration and production activities will be afforded, both domestically and in-country, and (vi) what other local laws the enterprise will be subject to for the duration of the activities in-country. The answers to all of these questions will have a significant impact on the strategy ultimately employed to undertake the exploration and production activities in the foreign jurisdiction. To ask them—and more—is prudent; to not ask them could be fatal to the viability of the project and, in the end, to the relationship with the client.

Key Areas of Risk

The financial implications of energy law all relate to the effective mitigation of project financing and development risks, as well as operational risks related to existing infrastructure investments such as plants, pipelines and vessels.

Price Risks

Most projects are begun, and financing is often sought, when commodity prices are high. Clearly, unexpected changes in underlying commodity prices can dramatically impact the future return of a project and, potentially, its fundamental viability. Companies need their lawyers to seek flexibility and contingencies in their contractual arrangements. Unfortunately, some companies lose sight of the considerable impact of price risk when the industry undergoes a period of sustained high prices such as current oil price levels. Other companies, mindful of bust periods, impose a very conservative pricing model when conducting cost/benefit analyses for significant investment strategies to mitigate against overly optimistic project champions. For example, some current LNG projects have stalled because supply agreements were not in place at the appropriate time or sufficient and reliable supply could not be obtained at a project-viable pricing level.

Geopolitical Risks

Assets purchased or deployed in politically unstable regions of the world pose significant risks for developers and investors. Recourse to arbitration, should assets be seized by a hostile government or become inaccessible as a function of armed conflict or other political unrest, is one key component of planning appropriate contingencies and mitigating risks implicit in such contracts. When there is the possibility of dispute between one's client and a governmental entity or a foreign counterparty, mitigating the risk that the client will be "hometowned" in that foreign jurisdiction is critical and the transactional lawyer who is cognizant of the risks and the means by which such risks are ameliorated is invaluable. In addition, contract language that ensures consistent application following subsequent changes in law and that ensures profits earned in foreign jurisdictions are capable of being repatriated to the client's jurisdiction of choice is of paramount import in any cross-border deal. Imagine the uncertainty attending a contract between a multinational company and a host government when the host government is unconstrained in its ability to legislate around its obligations in the contract. In effect, one party to the contract, acting in its capacity as a sovereign government, passes a law that makes its own performance under the contract illegal, thus providing an exit with impunity. Alternatively, suppose the host government doesn't make its performance of the contract illegal but instead passes legislation that precludes the multinational company from moving its payments—which are being made in a timely manner per the terms of the contract—out of the country. The result is the same in either case, and it is not a result with which the multinational will be pleased under any circumstances.

Timing Risks

Business interruption as a function of weather, accident or human error is very costly and the energy business is not immune to such concerns. Exploration and production projects depend on timely and reliable drilling equipment. Pipelines must transport hydrocarbons to markets where they are needed and processing plant disruptions have implications for entire communities and industries. Energy lawyers help companies mitigate and manage these risks and their downstream contractual and financial implications.

These risks, among others, are closely tied to—and are quite often impacted by—the concept of *force majeure* and the way *force majeure* is defined in the relevant contract. As a result, learning what to look for, what to insist upon, and what can be traded in a well-drafted and tailored *force majeure* clause is of paramount importance to the effective energy lawyer. That *force majeure* clauses are often considered boilerplate belies the importance of each word in this provision and the need to carefully tailor this provision to the facts and circumstances surrounding each transaction.

For example, will strikes and lockouts be an event of *force majeure* in a shipbuilding contract containing a very strict construction schedule to ensure that the vessel's delivery coincides with the start-up of production and receiving facilities? If so, will they be limited to some degree? Does it matter that the small country in which the shipyard is located is prone to prolonged and often violent labor disputes? Does it matter that a small delay in vessel delivery could cause millions of dollars in losses given the vessel's importance as an integral part of the project? Because the basic concept of *force majeure* is that performance is excused when prevented by an event beyond the control of the party claiming *force majeure* relief, it is troublesome to include strikes and lockouts within the definition when the strike or lockout could very well have been caused, in whole or in part, by the actions or inactions of the shipyard. Suppose the shipyard has in fact contributed to the labor dispute resulting in the strike and as a result is entitled to claim *force majeure* relief for late delivery. Suppose also that the vessel's late delivery causes export and import facilities to lie dormant when they should be fully operational and generating revenue for the project sponsors, and that the liquidated damages agreed upon in the shipbuilding contract for late delivery—which are meant in part to mitigate these losses—are no longer payable because the shipyard's non-performance is excused by *force majeure*. The careful lawyer will attempt to constrain or limit to some extent the ability of the shipyard to claim relief in this situation.

One approach that has been used successfully is to limit strikes to "general strikes" and, in so doing, give the shipyard the ability to claim relief only when a nationwide or industry-wide strike impacts its production schedule. Another approach is to limit the number of days during which relief will be granted for strikes, thereby putting a ceiling on the potential exposure flowing from this risk. At very least, this example illustrates that, in certain types of contracts, the typical definition of *force majeure* may have to be tailored to some degree. The careful and effective lawyer will recognize where this is the case and will craft a limitation that works within the facts and circumstances at play.

Common Challenges

When companies begin a new venture, particularly if that venture is in a new region of the world or a new part of the energy value chain, executives typically run the risk of underestimating (i) cultural and regulatory differences that cause unexpected delays or barriers to timely completion, (ii) planning processes that omit key stakeholders and regulatory bodies that can block or halt project planning, and (iii) economic business cases for project return on investment that do not consider the impact of regulatory compliance costs, commodity price and interest rate shifts in response to extraordinary events, and so on.

Involving counsel at the strategic level of a project and early in the planning process can avoid many, if not all, such challenges. If the project to be undertaken is in a previously uncharted jurisdiction where the project sponsor is concerned, retaining lead counsel in the sponsor's own jurisdiction and local counsel in the project's jurisdiction is often the best model for success. Lead counsel can help the company retain and effectively coordinate with local counsel. Lead counsel can also understand the regulatory terrain in complete detail prior to project start-up and help the project team manage the expectations of upper management, financial backers, and venture partners by bringing to bear knowledge of similar projects, similar circumstances, and the solutions that proved successful in such projects and circumstances.

One pitfall I see quite often among business developers and lawyers doing international deals for the first time is the proclivity to rely solely on local counsel when issues arise in the project country. As was illustrated above when discussing crossover issues among legal disciplines, the potential for issues to arise is acute and the potential number of issues are myriad. Effective lead counsel remains actively involved in the affairs that other, less experienced, lead counsel often cede to local counsel in their entirety. Depending on the project country and depth of the legal market in that jurisdiction, the risk inherent in this approach can be acute. Effective lead counsel will, whenever possible, take the lead in briefing the relevant issues under local law and using local counsel to verify their conclusions. In this way, lead counsel can bring to bear its own quality control protocols, thereby ensuring consistency and accuracy for the client and, at the same time, remaining in control of all moving parts involved in the transaction.

Critical Success Factors

First and foremost is a keen personal interest in the energy business. I believe that unless one is truly interested in the business, one cannot hope to come close to understanding its nuances, market dynamics, and standard practices. I began working in the oil business while in college, earning tuition money by moving drilling rigs off the lease upon completion of drilling. I think a keen interest in, and understanding of, the fundamentals of the business are an invaluable asset for the business advisor, regardless of the advisor's academic discipline. This is particularly true in the energy business, where there is a strong precedent for members of top management to come from engineering and technical backgrounds and to have had years of operational experience. These executives genuinely appreciate advisors who bring a broader view and a strong knowledge of their business to the table, as well as excellent legal skills.

I feel I am most successful when my involvement in a project occurs at an early stage, when the goals of the project are well understood by all stakeholders, and when the project team is open to allowing me to bring to bear personal experience with similar projects as well as the collective experience of my partners and my firm as an integrated team. One of the most frustrating things for a transactional lawyer is to be brought into a deal late in the game once the client and its counterparty are too far down the road to adequately and fairly consider alternative approaches.

Because energy is critical to firing the global economy and is a capital-intensive and highly technical field, I find that staying abreast of global developments, technological changes and market dynamics through attendance and participation at industry events is critical. I like to understand my clients' businesses up close and, whenever possible, I take opportunities to visit operational locations, to tour newly developed plants, and to observe demonstrations of newer technologies. The industry is changing rapidly and is global in scope, so the effective energy lawyer will try to keep abreast of new developments whenever possible.

Finally, I believe leveraging the full knowledge of my partners, to the extent that I can do so without breaching confidentiality, gives my clients the benefit of best practices, leading practice materials, and contractual precedents. I think in today's competitive and increasingly expensive legal market, every bit of leverage adds value.

The Art of Negotiation

Depending on the tenor of the negotiation and the level of cooperation or acrimony, the art of negotiation can take different tacks. If there is a cooperative, problem-solving approach to the negotiation, I believe I am far more productive when I take on the role of the inventive problem solver. While some lawyers simply identify issues, the effective lawyer also suggests corresponding solutions. The effective lawyer in this context asks himself or herself what can be done within the law to accommodate both parties, or to at least effect a compromise that affords the parties a chance to meet each other in the middle.

On the other hand, if the negotiation is particularly acrimonious, when possible the preferred approach is to come "loaded for bear." The most successful approach is to take a position that is supportable by hard facts, numbers if available, plausible scenarios describing risk, etc. As many expert negotiators will say, the golden rule in this case is to make your point, then shut your mouth. Human nature, when faced with silence, dictates that someone say something; therefore, making the other person say something in response to your position is a very effective technique. The more the other side talks, the greater the chance they will concede, even if incrementally. Often, clients ask their lawyers to advocate positions that are less than fully supportable with facts, numbers, or plausible scenarios. In such cases, while it is always a good idea to try to explain to the client the difficulty in advocating an untenable position, if unsuccessful in getting the client to change positions, find the strongest argument you've got and do the best you can.

I think it is imperative that the lawyer does not get personally involved or invested in a particular position. It is very difficult to be an effective advocate once objectivity is lost and one becomes personally invested in the issues under discussion. This ties in with my discussion above about keeping in mind that it is not the lawyer's decision to shoulder or reject a particular risk. It is the lawyer's job to fully identify the risk and, if the client decides to bear it, try to mitigate it to the extent possible. Getting personally invested makes the performance of this mandate very difficult and compromises the value of the lawyer to the client.

I consider my role on behalf of clients in a negotiation as that of their advocate. I also believe I bring additional experience and an objectivity that, at times, can help the client see the upside or downside of an opportunity or challenge that occurs during a negotiation.

There are many different players involved in a typical negotiation. The business developer or lead commercial representative usually leads the negotiations and is supported, both on an advocacy front and when matters of strictly legal significance arise, by the lawyer. In the energy context, there is typically an engineer present alongside the commercial developer. In addition, depending on the transaction, environmental and other regulatory personnel might be involved as well as financial advisors, accountants, and tax experts.

In preparing for a negotiation, understanding the facts is critical. I try to understand as much as possible about the industry sector, the geographic location, and any technology to be employed in getting the project off the ground. Without this background knowledge, it is often difficult—quite often impossible—to be able to put the contract in the proper context and perspective. That places the advocate, whether he or she is a lawyer or a commercial developer, at a significant disadvantage. Having the facts is indeed critical; it goes without saying that knowing the documents being negotiated is equally important.

Commonly Negotiated Items

The events occurring in the United States on September 11, 2001, in London on July 7, 2005, and in various other locations around the globe have added a new dimension to many energy negotiations as planning for security and business interruptions have come to the fore. When considering potential liabilities and business interruptions, it has become important to demonstrate that significant and reasonable measures are in place to make a plant, vessel, or other infrastructure site secure. For example, less than a year after September 11, 2001, lawyers engaged in transactions involving maritime transportation of hydrocarbons were forced to conceive of and agree upon new contract provisions allocating risks and duties under the hastily enacted and newly ratified International Ship and Port Facility Security Code (the ISPS Code). The ISPS Code mandates a number of notice and other requirements and threatens refusal of entry at ports around the world to non-compliant vessels carrying crude oil, LPG, LNG, petrochemicals and various other hydrocarbon products. Similarly, it has become important for project developers to consider a heightened risk that such events could impact a project's timely completion or their ability to honor supply contracts and other obligations, both upstream and downstream.

Other types of business interruptions resulting from transportation embargoes, vessel damage, adverse weather conditions, armed conflict and similar events generally come under the heading of *force majeure* and factor prominently in negotiations as well. Fossil fuels come from every corner of the globe, but the majority of fuel used in the world must be transported significant distances before it can be consumed. This exposes suppliers, transporters, and end users to a variety of uncertainties that lead to business risks. All of these will be the subject of careful negotiation in a well-crafted set of transaction documents.

Defining Success in Negotiation

I consider a negotiation successful not when my client gets everything he or she was seeking, but when he or she gets what is fair under the circumstances and the deal gets done. I don't subscribe to the slash-and-burn negotiation strategy where negotiation is a blitzkrieg, taking no prisoners. Nor do I think a war of attrition is productive as a negotiation strategy. To be sure, acrimony can arise, but I think the better approach to negotiation is to be a problem solver rather than a hired gun. As I've alluded to above, there is also the tendency among some lawyers to raise issues without proposing solutions. In this way, the legal profession has often suffered a bad reputation because we are looked at as impediments to consummating a deal rather than as facilitators. I believe the good lawyer is a facilitator, and a professional to whom the layman can look to find ways through the multitude of legal issues that arise in the typical energy transaction.

To summarize, I think the successful negotiator must be armed with a deep understanding of, and interest in, the client's business. He or she must have a keen understanding of the facts applicable in each transaction and the goals and objectives of the client. Without an understanding of the facts at play, one cannot hope to be an effective advocate. Similarly, unless I know where the client wants to go and what he or she wants to achieve in getting there, I can't hope to be successful on his or her behalf. He or she must also have a keen awareness of and an ability to avoid taking positions during a negotiation that are untenable. Advocating tenuous positions can lead only to a loss of credibility. When credibility is lost, advocating even the strongest of positions becomes more difficult. Know when to advise your client against such positions. Taking and ultimately conceding untenable positions will only make it more difficult to get what your client really wants—and has sound reasons for wanting—out of the negotiation.

Limiting the Client's Exposure

In my practice, financial exposure is quite often limited by the use of liquidated damages regimes and the disclaimer of consequential damages in the relevant documents. Furthermore, there are quite often local laws or international conventions that limit liability in certain contexts. In such cases, the client can get a pretty good indication of the total exposure at the contract negotiation stage. In contexts where liquidated damages are not employed contractually, it is more difficult to assess what actual damages for breach of contract might be. However, case law and statutory rules (in many foreign jurisdictions) often govern and/or shed considerable light on the imposition and extent of what actual damages for breach might be.

Suppose, for example, that a client decides, for reasons related to liability under local laws and international conventions applicable to vessel owners (but not charterers), to enter into a long-term time charter of an LNG tanker to bring LNG from Indonesia to Japan. The term of the charter is twenty years, and the hire to be paid on a daily basis (covering capital cost only and excluding operational costs attributable to the vessel) is equal to $55,000. Assume the client has some project risk associated with development of the upstream liquefaction facility and needs the flexibility to be able to walk away from the charter if the upstream facilities never get built. In such a case, I would suggest that the client attempt to obtain the contractual right to terminate the charter upon payment of a negotiated sum. Among other factors (including the value of the vessel at the time of the termination, the number of months or years remaining in the term of the charter upon termination, etc.), the amount of that termination payment would presumably bear some relationship to the amount of time the vessel owner believes it would reasonably take to find other employment for the vessel following termination. Thus, if the vessel owner thinks it likely that finding other suitable employment for the vessel would take up to twenty-four months following any termination, the parties might agree to a termination payment somewhere in the neighborhood of $40 million ($55,000 per day multiplied by 730 days equals $40,150,000). This is but one example—and, admittedly, an oversimplified example—of trying to minimize a client's liability under a transportation contract. Having such a limitation, however, might mean the difference between getting the project off the ground and having to walk away because the risk profile is too great.

Deal Breakers

Regulatory approvals have been very difficult for energy deals of late, especially in the United States. The two most recent examples of such difficulties are CNOOC's attempt to acquire Unocal and the current level of difficulty for permitting and siting LNG facilities on U.S. shores. Clearly, environmental and conservationist concerns and their impact on regulatory approvals are still one of the biggest hurdles to energy project development. The following two examples are illustrative of the types of issues that, while not commercial in nature, can be just as much a deal killer as the parties' inability to agree upon price, delivery schedule or other terms traditionally regarded as deal killers. Drawing again on my own experience in the LNG business, the two examples below are LNG projects that saw their demise on the heels of insurmountable regulatory hurdles.

LNG in California

In 1973, Pacific Gas & Electric and Pacific Lighting Company, through a joint venture they called Western Liquefied Natural Gas Terminal Associates (WLNG), sought approval to build an LNG receiving and regasification terminal on the California coast. Initially, WLNG proposed Los Angeles, Oxnard and Point Conception as three alternate sites for the planned facility. The California Coastal Commission, the California Public Utilities Commission and the California Energy Commission all had a role in the approval process and, because of a difference in the mandate given each agency, all had differing views on the major issues presented by the proposal. What resulted was an inter-agency dispute that ultimately undermined the entire approval process—not only at the state level but federally as well, because the California Public Utility Commission and the California Energy Commission appeared during the permitting process before the Federal Power Commission (now the Federal Energy Regulatory Commission) and failed to present a united position on the facility.

After more than three years following the initial request for approval, WLNG was faced with an impasse. What followed was a massive lobbying effort on the part of WLNG that resulted in the passage, in the California state legislature, of the California LNG Terminal Siting Act of 1977. This piece of legislation wrested ultimate approval authority from the California Coastal Commission and gave it to the California Public Utility Commission, but provided that the Coastal Commission was to select and rank a number of proposed sites, in cooperation with the potential developer.

WLNG, relying on a provision in the legislation that allowed selection of a site for the Public Utility Commission's consideration even if it had previously been rejected by the Coastal Commission, chose Point Conception. However, a U.S. district court had already determined that Point Conception didn't meet the Federal Energy Regulatory Commission's seismic siting criteria due to the presence of fault lines. As a result of federal opposition to Point Conception and the opposition and inter-agency disputes that arose in connection with the other proposed sites, WLNG abandoned its proposal more than eight years after initial applications were filed.

LNG in Italy

The Italian state electric utility, ENEL, decided in 1996 not to build an LNG receiving terminal on the coast of Tuscany and attempted to cancel its LNG sales contract with Nigeria LNG Ltd. The impetus behind ENEL's cancellation was not merely a desire by ENEL to build elsewhere or simply to get out of its deal with Nigeria LNG, but significant difficulties in the permitting process culminating in a veto of the proposed site and an alternate site by a newly elected and more environmentally active Italian government. What resulted was a breach of contract suit against ENEL for damages in excess of $13 billion.

While ENEL claimed the *force majeure* clause of the contract afforded relief from its obligations thereunder as a result of the government veto—an event arguably beyond ENEL's control—the merits of that argument were never decided upon because the case was settled and the parties agreed that Nigerian LNG would be shipped to France instead of Italy, in exchange for Russian gas diverted to Italy by French buyers.

What this case highlights, however, and what ENEL's argument implicitly suggests, is that *force majeure* provisions in such contracts should contemplate the permitting process, the expenses associated with securing permits and other governmental authorizations, and the potential inability to go forward with the project due to a failure to obtain such permits and authorizations. In addition, it suggests that prudent lawyers should advise their clients to condition the effectiveness of key contracts on the successful procurement of such permits and authorizations.

Fowl Play

The Italian experience highlighted above illustrates yet another difficulty in consummating transactions in the energy sector: lining up all of the elements in the supply chain within the timeframe required to get all pieces in place. Again, bringing to bear my own experience in the LNG industry, it is not difficult to appreciate the unique challenges involved in bringing a project to fruition. Bringing LNG into a new regasification facility requires marine transportation. However, few project sponsors will sign a long-term charter for a fleet of vessels, purchase a fleet of vessels, or order a fleet of newbuild vessels before they know there will be LNG to transport to the regasification facility. Thus, the transportation link is dependent upon the supply link. Similarly, the regasification link will not get built unless there is a secure supply, ships to transport that supply, and long-term, creditworthy off-takers who are contractually bound to take the regasified LNG. In order to secure supply, project sponsors either need to build a liquefaction plant or secure some other source of supply through a long-term sale and purchase agreement for LNG produced in an existing liquefaction plant. But going further upstream, project sponsors cannot build the liquefaction plant unless they have in place long-term gas sale agreements providing feedstock gas for liquefaction, and such agreements often need to be negotiated with host governments as part of concession agreements or production sharing contracts. Furthermore, it would be difficult to obtain financing on a liquefaction plant without having long-term LNG sale and purchase agreements in place with off-takers who commit to supply the regasification facility via the shipping link. As you can see, there is a bit of a chicken-and-egg conundrum—a bit of fowl play, as I like to put it—in all of this. Indeed, projects of this nature are complicated and the failure or delay in one link of the chain can have a detrimental effect on the viability of the project as a whole.

Conclusion

Success for lawyers in the energy sector requires the same general skills that breed success in any field of law. In this way, there's nothing magic about energy law or energy lawyers. Success requires hard work, attention to detail, a deep base of knowledge about the field (or at least a willingness to acquire such knowledge), a keen interest in the industry, and a thorough understanding of the law applicable to the particular circumstances surrounding the transaction.

The energy lawyer must have a sense of adventure, because he or she may find himself or herself on nearly every continent from one month to the next. Among today's lawyers who find themselves globetrotting on a regular basis, the energy lawyer features prominently because geology is no respecter of political boundaries, nor is it influenced by proximity to major markets. This brings unique challenges and affords equally unique opportunities. The successful energy lawyer relishes both.

Kevin Keenan is a partner in the global projects practice at Akin Gump Strauss Hauer & Feld LLP. Mr. Keenan is based in the firm's Houston office and focuses primarily on the development of hydrocarbon reserves by public and private entities acting alone or as participants in various joint venture arrangements. Mr. Keenan has significant experience with energy-related transactions and has played a key role in negotiating and documenting the long-term purchase and sale of crude oil, crude oil products, natural gas and LNG. His work has also included project development of crude oil refining and LNG-related infrastructure in the United States, Aruba, The Bahamas, and the United Kingdom. In addition, he has played a key role in the negotiation and consummation of numerous time and voyage charters with respect to LNG tankers and contracts for the construction of LNG tankers in South Korean shipyards. He also assists clients in a wide range of core business areas, including mergers, acquisitions, and divestitures. While these transactions typically involve players in the energy industry, they have, from time to time, involved other industry segments as well.

Apart from the transactions with which Mr. Keenan has been involved in the United States and those international transactions mentioned above, he has also been lead counsel or played key roles in transactions involving energy-related assets in Angola, Argentina, Belgium, Canada, Côte d'Ivoire, Egypt, Equatorial Guinea, Greece, Indonesia, Japan, Kuwait, Mexico, Nigeria, Norway, Qatar, Uruguay and Vietnam. Mr. Keenan has given numerous speeches and presentations around the world and has published articles in a number of industry journals in North America, Europe, Asia, and the Middle East. His writings and presentations cover a range of issues from assessing and mitigating the risks of modern maritime piracy as it relates to the transportation of hydrocarbons to the nuts and bolts of project development and supply chain risk management. One of his primary areas of interest, especially because it often overlaps with the sea-bound transportation of hydrocarbons, is the multitude of binding liability limitations afforded to vessel owners and charterers by international conventions, local laws, and novel contractual arrangements.

Mr. Keenan earned his J.D. from Georgetown University Law Center and his B.A., with high honors, from Idaho State University.

Energy Law: Peeling Back the Layers

James M. Avery
Partner
Brown Rudnick Berlack Israels LLP

Navigating the Energy Regulatory Commission

Due to the complexity and unusual structure of energy law, it is imperative that the attorney practicing in this area understand two fundamental principles. First, the practitioner should appreciate the unique position of the regulatory commission within the government. The public utility commission does not fit neatly into any single branch of the government, but rather is a hybrid of the judiciary, executive, and legislative branches. The commissioners are typically appointed by and serve at the pleasure of the executive. These commissioners also serve a quasi-judicial function and are bound by substantial administrative procedure regulations and requirements. At the same time, particularly in terms of rate setting, these commissioners are performing a legislative function, implementing authority expressly reserved to the legislative branch. The so-called "filed rate doctrine," where equitable defenses are not available with respect to rate matters, is a prime example of the nature of the utility commissioner's legislative authority. Thus, approved rates are effectively treated as a legislative act although approved by executive officials after a quasi-judicial process.

This unique structure must be remembered in order to be successful, whether representing a utility, an electric generator, or a customer. For this reason, the trial attorney who practices energy law with the belief that the rules of evidence and procedure are strictly applied at a utility commission will not always be successful; he or she must also be politically astute. Similarly, the politically minded attorney cannot lose sight of the fact that a compelling case must be presented to the agency that must apply established standards on a consistent basis. Negotiations of a contract that is subject to commission review in this area must reflect the varying factors influencing utility commissions, from strict adherence to precedent to the influences of political pressure on the issue of the day. The successful energy law attorney should therefore have an understanding of all the relevant technical issues, as well as the politics of the process. The best chance for success in energy proceedings, in sum, is through a cross-disciplinary approach.

The second fundamental principle is that the one constant in the field is change. This continuing tension in the field of energy law is most likely a consequence of the hybrid nature of the public utility commission. Thus, there is a continual shift between regulatory and market forces as the best means to address the particular issue of the day. The more recent trend has been a move toward greater reliance upon the market and less rigorous or light-handed regulation. This could change in the face of higher market prices or concerns about reliability not being addressed pursuant to emerging "market rules." Thus, the political response to price spikes in the aftermath of the hurricanes of 2005 or reliability concerns may well be to move away from a more market-driven energy market and more towards traditional, central planning. Similarly, the greater deference to market forces that has facilitated more frequent utility mergers may eventually be reversed if customers or local politicians feel a loss of influence and control over traditionally regulated entities. The successful practitioner must sense the current state of tension between market and regulation and act accordingly. For longer-term projects or agreements, the successful practitioner must build in flexibility to address a range of outcomes along this spectrum.

The practitioner must be mindful that there are typically several layers to energy regulation, and a corresponding tension that allows markets and regulators to function symbiotically. The entire basis of the successful relationship between markets and regulators is founded upon the accepted existence of monopolies in the energy industry. Historically, monopolies have been in existence at the state level from the earliest times that certain of these services were commercially available. This was primarily due to the degree of difficulty inherent in allowing multiple utility or energy companies to compete for customers in a single community, particularly with respect to the logistical issues of multiple power lines, telephone poles, or gas mains in the same area.

By allowing a single energy company to establish itself within an area and then placing regulatory strictures regarding rates and reliability upon that business, the policymakers have been able to ensure that services critical to the public's health and safety are consistently available at the lowest cost possible for the consumer. As time has passed, environmental guidelines have been instituted as well, necessitating that in addition to the priorities of low rates and exceptional reliability, energy is delivered to the consumer with as little impact on the environment as possible.

This balance of cost, environment, and reliability concerns has become a standard by which utilities now function at the retail level. There have, however, been quite different views on the best way to further these goals, with many policymakers believing market structures were better able to achieve these objectives. For example, the federal government was charged with regulating energy markets at the wholesale level; for example, the rates for delivering natural gas through pipelines from the production area to the utility were regulated by the U.S. government. The belief that competition could potentially lower energy costs motivated the government to deregulate the delivery of energy and retail at the wholesale levels in the past twenty to thirty years. While this effort has largely been perceived as successful for many customers, the lack of strict regulatory guidelines results in many customers being subject to the forces of the market. These markets have often been particularly volatile, an example being the natural gas markets since 2000. This regime is more likely to result in immediate higher costs for the consumer whenever energy resources are limited, whether through political events or natural disasters like Hurricane Katrina and more rapid price decreases in time of excess supply. Traditional regulation may result in less price volatility but may also result in higher overall costs. The successful practitioner must understand and consider not only where the balance between regulation and market forces is at the moment, but also where the balance is likely to be in the future.

In sum, these two fundamental principles of the energy practice need to be addressed regardless of the type of project you are addressing. Energy regulators are always seeking to balance their obligation to strictly apply established rules and precedent, and the goal of responding to political forces. They must also balance the tension between markets and regulation. These factors affect success in rate matters, resource planning, facility development, and contracting practices. Several tactics can and should be employed to achieve success.

The Importance of Effective Communication

In order to be a successful practitioner of energy law and address the identified principles, effective communication at all levels is essential. A sound technical or evidentiary case must be presented in any regulatory proceeding, but effective "political" communication with the appropriate audience must also be pursued. When attempting to develop a project that will potentially benefit customers over a broad area, the communication process should begin as early as possible in order to limit difficulties going forward. This may be accomplished by scheduling informal meetings with community or consumer groups, as well as regulators who will be reviewing the project at a later stage of development. Such stakeholder processes are increasingly relied upon to address political forces. Ideally, these discussions should be initiated before a site for a planned energy project has been chosen or paperwork filed, in order to ensure that the project is feasible before investing undue time or funds.

For example, in working with a client on developing a site for a liquefied natural gas facility recently, we were able to complete a major state regulatory administrative proceeding in approximately six months, moving from "petition" to "commission" of the facility within one year. This process typically may require years of negotiation and discussion. However, by working with town officials informally, state legislators, and energy regulators on issues of concern, the client was able to avoid a number of common obstacles and complete the project expeditiously. In addition, several of the ideas that were incorporated into the design of the facility were generated during discussions with town officials.

Communication is equally important in contracting. The attorney needs an understanding of the client's objectives and should seek to offer creative solutions. For example, our firm was representing a utility in negotiating a contract with a power plant developer. Such developers typically seek a return on investment relatively quickly, while this particular utility was more accustomed to working with a more extended timeline for its investments. By negotiating a contract in which there was little initial cost to the developer for the necessary utility service in the first years of the project, we were able to negotiate terms in which both parties saw substantial profits over the course of two decades in very different market/regulatory regimes.

Striking the Appropriate Balance: A Case Study

From the perspective of the client or consumer, a successful energy attorney needs to implement a strategy that balances the struggle between regulatory and market forces. Utilities are more familiar with this balance; other parties such as consumers need to catch up. The energy markets have been particularly volatile in recent years; as a result, most U.S. consumers have concerns about both the cost and reliability of their energy. To the extent regulators are stepping back to let market forces work, customers may need to take ownership of their own energy requirements and plan and act for their own best interests. Many customers, used to the traditionally paternalistic role of the utility, fail to act. There are a number of strategies that may be employed in order to empower today's energy consumer, including analyzing utility rate structures to be certain the customer takes the best service and conducts its operations accordingly, attempting to be more efficient in the ways energy is utilized within the business, and ensuring that energy is delivered by the entity offering the most cost-effective services.

For the business consumer, the energy attorney may need to emphasize practical business solutions that address energy requirements. For example, businesses should consider structuring operations in such a way as to ensure that production runs are performed in a manner that reflects energy cost causation. This is helpful, because many utility companies have what is known as a "demand rate," which means charges are based upon the highest level of energy delivered to the consumer over the course of a month. Regardless of whether this rate is retained for fifteen minutes or a week, the consumer will pay that rate for the entire month. By limiting production runs so this demand rate is managed, a business greatly reduces the amount of energy consumed and, thus, the cost of its energy bills.

In addition, businesses may consider building energy generation facilities on site, guaranteeing a potentially reliable source of power for operations and a possible reduction in costs. However, a business wishing to build such a facility must first examine siting issues, space availability, safety concerns, and contractual questions regarding how energy will be generated. For many, this analysis will demonstrate substantial benefits.

Ultimately, while there are more options for individual and business consumers with respect to the types of energy services and companies available, there are also a number of questions that must be considered in this politically charged economic climate. The consumer with the ability to objectively examine all options and use energy efficiently is the consumer who will save the most in the short and long term. Whatever strategy is pursued, an effective energy attorney will negotiate protective provisions for his or her client to address inevitable change. A longer-term contract must hold up under a range of regulatory conditions.

Remaining Competitive in Energy Law

While it was once common for individuals to spend much of their lives devoted to a single component of energy law, today it is more likely that professionals will periodically migrate from one area of the industry to another, often following changes in the market. Simply put, an attorney may need to reinvent himself or herself periodically. As regulatory policy changes, new skill sets need to be added.

The need to reinvent oneself is a consequence of the regular rejection of market rules. Policies and trends are often reactionary in the energy industry. For example, in the 1960s and 1970s, nuclear power became highly fashionable; as a result, nuclear plants were almost exclusively the type of energy facilities being built during that period of time. When safety and cost concerns became an issue, there was a rapid decline in building, and today development of such plants is virtually nonexistent. Practitioners in this area moved on to new areas.

In the early 1990s, after some overbuilding and in the early steps of competition in the generation market, there was a movement toward integrated system planning. The movement toward competition required an understanding of a range of sophisticated financing and hedging strategies. Thus, a greater understanding of complex physical and financial instruments was necessary.

One of the most effective ways to achieve success as an energy attorney is to stay connected. This will keep you tuned into the current state of regulation and the likely future trends. There are a variety of ways to stay involved, from attending certain key industry conferences to bar association activities. By maintaining contact with individuals already practicing in the area and developing these same connections in emerging areas, the energy attorney has a greater ability to continue to achieve success in the industry.

Achieving Success as an Energy Law Attorney

Ultimately, the attorney specializing in energy law must be a master analyst and communicator in a number of forums. He or she must recognize the role politics plays in the energy industry, while simultaneously having a strong knowledge base of the regulatory laws and legal proceedings pertaining to energy. The practitioner must also understand how markets and changes to market rules affect decisions. There must be a facility for working with individuals ranging from general contractors to federal regulators, and further there must be recognition of the value each of these individuals brings to the process. The successful attorney must also recognize the need for new skill sets and draw upon them. The attorney with the ability to understand and communicate the vast number of intricacies and eccentricities inherent in energy law is most likely to achieve success in the field.

James Avery has represented a variety of clients in a wide range of regulatory proceedings before the Massachusetts Department of Telecommunications and Energy and the Massachusetts Energy Facilities Siting Board. Mr. Avery has also represented clients in a variety of commercial and financial transactions, including acquisitions, mergers, corporate restructuring, contracts, and financings.

Examples of recent matters include: representation of a gas utility in an innovative performance-based rate proceeding resulting in the approval of a ten-year rate plan; representation of a gas utility in securing the necessary regulatory and environmental approvals for the first liquefied natural gas facility in Massachusetts in over twenty-five years and the permanent financing of the facility; representation of an electric utility in the siting of a new electric transmission line; representation of a publicly traded public utility holding company in a merger; representation of numerous customers in electric and natural gas procurement and contract negotiation; representation of a gas utility in structuring and securing necessary approvals for a commodity portfolio optimization alliance with other utilities and a major natural gas producer; and representation of energy clients in long-term debt and equity financings, including project financings.

Mr. Avery recently contributed a chapter on the Department of Public Utilities (now the Department of Telecommunications and Energy) to the Lawyers Cooperative Publishing Compilation on Massachusetts Procedure, *Volume 9, and he was a contributor to* State and Federal Deregulation of Electric and Natural Gas Services in Massachusetts, *published by the National Business Institute.*

Mr. Avery is a member of the Massachusetts and Boston Bar Associations, and he was a member of Governor Romney's outage preparedness task force investigation of the August 14, 2003, power outage.

Preparing for and Succeeding in Negotiations

Chad Mills

Partner

Locke Liddell & Sapp LLP

The Role of an Energy Lawyer

The most predominant components of energy law are commercial law, bankruptcy law, and state and federal regulatory law. My work as an energy lawyer falls into three categories. First, I help companies that are trying to develop and finance energy infrastructure projects. Recently, a large portion of this work has related to the development of receiving terminals to import liquefied natural gas (LNG) into North America. Second, I help companies buy and sell energy infrastructure assets such as power plants, pipelines, and LNG receiving terminals. Third, I work with companies that are buying and selling energy commodities such as natural gas, electricity, and LNG, as well as with companies that are buying and selling financial derivatives instruments based on the value of energy commodities.

I believe transactional lawyers can add the most value for our clients by helping each client bring its goals into sharp focus and then ensuring that the transaction is documented in a way that will achieve these goals.

The Financial Implications of Energy Law

Long-term energy contracts often require significant commitments of capital and resources over long periods of time. In these types of transactions, a slight misunderstanding in the contract can lead one party or the other to great unhappiness at some point during the deal.

For example, consider a large, but not unusual, long-term LNG purchase and sale agreement. Under this type of agreement, the buyer might agree to purchase LNG equating to 100 billion cubic feet of natural gas each year for twenty years. In some cases, the buyer may agree to a "take-or-pay" provision, where the buyer would agree to pay for the LNG whether it is taken or not (subject only to seller's failure and *force majeure*). Gas prices under these types of contracts are typically tied to a market-based index. If the gas price averages $7/MMBtu over this period of time, the buyer is committing to spend $700,000,000 each year, for a total of $14 billion over the life of the contract. In a contract of this size, the significance of the details is staggering. For example, a tiny negotiating concession in the measurement provisions could result in a difference worth tens of millions pf dollars over the life of the contract.

Common Client Mistakes

No deal is ever perfect. There are, however, specific mistakes I see repeated frequently among clients, regardless of their situations.

First, a client should not wait until midway through negotiations in a transaction to start thinking about the counterparty's credit. This should always be the very first question the client asks: which legal entity is on the hook for this contract, and how creditworthy is that entity? I can never stress enough to clients that it matters very little what the contract says if the other side is not creditworthy. It is also necessary to be extremely specific about who the exact counterparty will be. I advise clients to establish as early as possible that they want the ultimate parent company on the contract or as a guarantor.

Second, I believe clients should involve outside lawyers extremely early in the negotiating process. Even if the lawyer is only allowed to do a very cursory review of a heads of agreement or similar deal outline, this can be helpful in identifying large problems before they become entrenched in the deal structure.

A third common error is that energy companies in general fail to give enough thought to strategic considerations in the deal-making process itself. Few companies develop a game plan for how a transaction will be negotiated and, instead, simply react as circumstances arise. Having a game plan allows a company to react quickly and consistently during negotiations.

Adding Value for Clients: Elements of the Attorney's Role that Are Critical to Client Success

As an energy lawyer, I add value for my clients by trying to resolve negotiation deadlocks with creative solutions. Often, the parties feel as if they are miles apart, simply because they misunderstand one another's respective positions. By discussing alternative solutions, even if they are not ultimately adopted, the parties can learn what their true desires are and consider reasonable ways to achieve them.

The single most important factor in determining whether I am successful with a client is a willingness on the part of the client to give adequate consideration to overall strategy for the negotiation. It is a virtually insurmountable challenge to work successfully with clients who are reticent or unwilling to compromise. My ability to keep my edge in this field is also critical to my success as an energy lawyer. In order to stay on top of emerging knowledge, I read a number of trade publications (including *Platts LNG Daily*, *Platts Gas Daily*, *Platts Megawatt Daily*, and *Upstream*), and I frequently attend industry conferences. I also keep up with acquaintances in the industry at various companies, since networking and dynamic conversations with colleagues is an excellent way to stay abreast of current information and trends in the field.

The Art of Negotiation

The elements of any negotiation consist of preparation, education, leverage, emotion, and style. How these elements are used varies greatly, as each transaction is truly unique.

First, the lawyer and client should prepare as extensively as possible, given their resources and the size of the transaction. Ideally, this would involve:

- Determining the exact desired outcome of the negotiation. Surprisingly, given the importance of this objective, this is rarely done in advance.
- Developing a comprehensive strategy for how the negotiation itself should proceed.
- Gaining a thorough understanding of the marketplace for the type of transaction being negotiated. Interestingly, the most productive negotiations seem to occur between parties that have both prepared extensively for the negotiation. While this may seem counterintuitive, rarely is a lawyer or his or her client well served by ignorance or lack of preparation by the counterparty. Usually, a counterparty that is ill-prepared will simply take unreasonable positions.

Second, the negotiating parties should educate one another about their desired outcomes and their rationales for those desired outcomes. This is usually done through iterative oral discussions and written draft agreements.

Preparing for and Succeeding in Negotiations

It is this part of the process that most people identify as "negotiation," and as such, it is often viewed as unnecessary friction brought about by the parties' mutual greed or competitive instincts. There is some truth to this; however, I prefer to see this as a cooperative effort that, if properly used, can provide a transaction with the most collective utility.

Third, the client and his or her lawyer should understand which party has leverage on the various points of negotiation. If the other side has something your client desperately desires, and the other side has little immediate need for what your client has to offer, they will dictate the terms on almost all points, guided only by morality and the fear that the tables may be reversed in some future transaction. Fortunately, this is rarely the case. Generally, the field is more evenly balanced and may even change during the course of negotiations.

Fourth, it is critical to accept that emotion plays an important role in all negotiations. We are all human and therefore susceptible to fear, pride, anger, friendship, greed, regret, and similar feelings. Approaching the negotiating table with only cold rationality is simply impossible and probably not at all desirable. It is, however, important to know your—and your counterparty's—emotional weak spots. A lawyer should never allow emotion to take control. If your counterparty does so, this is usually an opportunity to gain an advantage for your client. A very common failing in this regard, particularly among lawyers, is pride. Time and time again, I see lawyers in negotiations who are more interested in proving their own mental prowess or legal skills than in obtaining the best outcome for their clients. Another common failing, chiefly falling on clients, is fear, though it is often not recognized as such. The most common type of fear that surfaces among clients is apprehension over losing the deal. Certainly, there is an ever-present risk of pressing too hard, resisting too much, or overplaying your hand in such a way that the counterparty determines to seek an alternative deal. However, when fear of losing the deal outweighs fear of entering into a bad deal, the client is hopelessly lost. In many situations, patience and resolve, rather than concessions, are the best cures for a difficult issue.

Finally, a lawyer must determine the most appropriate style to present for a given transaction, as there is no one-size-fits-all style. At times, a lawyer may need to appear demanding, while at others he or she may need to be

49

conciliatory. In some cases, openness and forthrightness are key, while other cases may require a lawyer to obfuscate to some degree. Of utmost importance, however, is remaining true to your own personality and principles. A lawyer should never pretend to be something he or she is not, as this will quickly unravel. For example, a demanding and imperious lawyer should never attempt a friendly and gregarious manner in negotiations, as no one will be convinced of its authenticity, and it will be perceived that the lawyer is trying to hide something. The lawyer would be better served by simply toning down his or her manner if the situation calls for a friendly approach. Everyone involved in negotiations should understand his or her own personality, including how it is viewed by others, and work flexibly within the boundaries of this personality to adapt to the demands of a particular transaction.

The Roles of Those Involved in Negotiations

As an energy lawyer, my role in the negotiation process varies dramatically depending on the transaction and the parties involved. Ultimately, the client determines what role I will play and, provided that I feel the client understands what it is doing and I am comfortable professionally and ethically with the role I am being asked to play, I will comply with the client's wishes. If the client is experienced in the particular type of negotiation and desires to control the process explicitly, I will function as a private counselor and draftsman. If the client wants to be involved but does not want to fully lead the process, I will act in a more direct role with the counterparty. In some cases, the client may express a desired outcome and direct me to take all the necessary steps to achieve that outcome.

The key players involved in negotiations vary greatly depending on the type of transaction. In any case, it is extremely important to identify, as early as possible, each of the various constituencies that have an interest in the outcome of the negotiations and how these constituencies need to be involved. Simplistically, you have two constituencies: your side and the other side. Obviously, it is never that simple. For example, the following groups, each with its own opinion and agenda, may fall under the umbrella of "your side": your primary commercial contact at the client, your primary legal contact at the client, your commercial contact's boss, your legal contact's boss, your client's operations group, your client's accounting department, your client's risk management department, your client's outside financial advisor, your client's board of directors, and others. In most deals, there is at least as much internal negotiation on each side as there is direct negotiation between the parties. Depending on the type of transaction, anyone might be a key player at some point in the process.

Preparing for Negotiations

I prepare for negotiations by trying to learn as much as possible about my client's desired outcome and strategy for achieving this outcome. I also research thoroughly the market for similar transactions and the people who will be involved in the transaction for my client and the counterparty. In learning about the marketplace, I find it is extremely important to delve into the details of similar transactions, if these details are available, and to understand where the similar transactions differ from the transaction at hand, both at the macro and micro levels. This is useful for arguing whether commercial precedent should or should not apply for any particular issue. It is surprising how often lawyers will cite precedent without understanding the context for the cited transaction.

The Most Often Negotiated Items When Discussing Energy Deals or Contracts

Very broadly speaking, the two most negotiated items in any energy contract are the consideration provided by each party and risk allocation. It is impossible to talk about these items separately, as they are intricately linked.

In many industries, it is probably simple to identify the consideration each party has provided under a contract. This is not always straightforward in complex energy transactions. These transactions often involve the exchange of cash, products, and services over time, and the types of exchanges may vary depending on certain contingencies. In some cases, we have difficulties even naming a contract because the combination of subject matter has never before been addressed. In these cases, the lawyer must go to great pains to ensure that the parties have a meeting of the minds regarding what is being purchased and sold; further, the contract must accurately reflect this meeting of the minds.

Very closely linked to consideration is how various risks are allocated under the contract. These negotiations typically manifest themselves in discussions on insurance and indemnity, representations and warranties, and events of default. All of these discussions involve specifying each party's rights and obligations upon the occurrence of contingent future events or discovery of unknown past events. Fortunately, many of the debates around how certain risks are allocated have been settled by long-standing commercial practice. There is usually a significant amount of room, however, around the edges of these settled debates to take up a great portion of the negotiating schedule. My job as my client's representative is to ensure that the client understands how these risks are allocated and to convince the counterparty to take as much of this risk as the deal, commercial precedent, and morality allow. Each side should carefully consider the link between the amount of risk it is being asked to bear and the exchange of consideration it is offered. The assumption or retention of risk is itself a very important form of consideration.

Advice for Clients with Respect to Negotiations in Energy Law

My favorite piece of advice in energy negotiations, or any negotiations for that matter, is to never be afraid to walk away from a bad deal, and to make sure the other side knows you are willing to do so. Remember, however, that it is virtually impossible to convince someone you are willing to walk away if it is not true. Something will give you away eventually, and the other side will go for blood. Make sure you actually keep other options open for consideration, including doing nothing at all. Be consistent and firm in your message about significant deal points, but never say "never" unless you really mean it.

Chad Mills is an attorney practicing in the areas of energy transactions, with a particular focus on energy project development and finance, mergers and acquisitions involving energy companies and assets, liquid natural gas transactions, and physical and derivative transactions involving natural gas and power. He has extensive experience with transactions involving natural gas and liquid natural gas, including sale and purchase agreements, gas transportation agreements, shipping and scheduling arrangements, and terminal services agreements.

Winning Strategies before the FERC

Sara Schotland

Partner

Cleary, Gottlieb, Steen & Hamilton

Role of an Energy Lawyer

The role of an energy lawyer is to help the client succeed with its application, regulatory filing, litigation, or transaction in an environment where there are multiple regulators. This means the energy lawyer can't be a narrow specialist, but must take into account the viewpoints of federal and state energy regulators, anti-trust regulators, state regulatory commissions, the Department of Energy, other federal regulators, and sometimes international authorities. In a utility acquisition, for example, all bases must be covered, and it is as important to obtain prompt approval from all regulators, requiring coordinated strategy and an integrated team.

The Federal Energy Regulatory Commission (FERC) regulates wholesale power transactions and transmission of power in interstate commerce. Since all of the lower forty-eight states are connected to the interstate grid except for Texas, the FERC's jurisdictional mandate is substantial. Understanding FERC regulation is a necessary but not sufficient condition for an energy lawyer. The energy lawyer has to have a working knowledge of the basics of state utility regulation and be smart enough to know what he or she doesn't know and work with local counsel.

Today's energy companies and energy-related transactions are affected not only by the regulators but also by the rules of the road established by regional transmission organizations (RTOs) and other operators of the transmission grid. It is important to follow the changing regimes and market structures implemented by each of these RTOs. Soon an electricity reliability organization (ERO) will be in place with its own set of rules and inspections and enforcement authorities. Developments should be followed nationwide. The regime implemented in the PJM region today will be followed in New England, New York, or the Midwest next month.

A key characteristic of energy regulation that differentiates it from other regulatory fields is that it is constantly in flux. In part, this is because the technical and economic issues associated with reliable and equitable operation of the electricity grid are highly complex; there are no easy answers. Also, there are a large number of stakeholders with competing and evolving agendas. In this environment, the energy lawyer must devote considerable attention to tracking regulatory and legislative developments at the federal and state level, to inform clients of proceedings in which they should participate to promote their interests, and to identify long-term trends that may present clients with business opportunities.

A client needs help on all aspects of the transaction, including antitrust, securities, and corporate law issues. An important role of the energy lawyer is to spot the issues that are likely to arise in connection with transactions.

Success before the FERC

Suggestions for clients in FERC proceedings include:

1. *Recognize that FERC policy changes with each commission.* While all agencies and commissions change their policies to some degree when their leadership is changed, FERC policy changes dramatically depending on the identity of the commissioner. Having observed the transitions from Hesse to Hebert to Wood to Kelliher, I have come to appreciate that last year's policy on whether RTO membership will be required or last year's policy on market power analysis in merger proceedings can be obsolete.

2. *Meet with the FERC.* Before a significant transaction is planned, it is a good idea to meet with the senior policy staff and the commissioners. The FERC is a very accessible agency. The commissioners and staff will meet with stakeholders and potential applicants on short notice. One needs to come to these meetings well prepared. The focus of the meeting should be on key policy issues presented by the application that are unique and not resolved by precedent. Once the application is filed, *ex parte* rules will kick in and meetings will not be possible unless the application is uncontested.

Meetings with FERC staff are as important as meetings "on the eleventh floor" with the commissioners. FERC staff is very knowledgeable. I think it is a mistake to meet with the commissioners before exchanging views with staff. Often, it is useful to meet with the general counsel, for example, with respect to applications for declaratory order on jurisdictional issues, or initiatives involving FERC implementation of its new authority under recent energy legislation.

3. *Marshal your allies.* Advocacy before the FERC, like lobbying before Congress, is most successful when your client doesn't stand alone. Sometimes competitors can be allies—for example, for bank clients we obtained waivers from power marketing precedent that would otherwise have precluded bank entry into power marketing. A single bank might not have been able to achieve this result; several banks working together demonstrated the need for relief for the industry. In numerous proceedings, we have found that public power or state consumer advocates will support our clients' positions in favor of restructuring.

4. *Take credible positions.* A frequent mistake in FERC meetings and filings is to advocate positions that are impractical because they would involve not just a change in FERC policy, but deviating from express statutory language, which the FERC is required to follow. It is also pointless to try to persuade the commission to adopt an oversight policy incompatible with the commission's resources. Advocate a position that makes sense not only for your client but also as a matter of commission precedent in future cases.

5. *Raise concerns as early as possible in a proceeding.* It is easier to influence FERC policy before they issue a notice of proposed rule-making than after. It is easier to persuade the FERC to take a certain result during the initial intervention period than on rehearing of a final decision. It is a false economy to wait and see interim results: advocate the client's policy position early before the commission has committed itself to a contrary position.

6. *Support the commission.* Often, companies benefit from a commission policy they regard as well considered. A common mistake is to take comfort in a favorable passage in a notice of proposed rule-making and not weigh in during the comment period against those who will argue for its removal. When the FERC has adopted a sensible proposal, weigh in to commend that proposal in the rule-making process so the FERC has support in the record. Similarly, in court cases, consider intervening on the side of the FERC when the decision is favorable to the company and is being challenged on judicial review.

7. *Adopt a courteous tone.* Be courteous and respectful in interactions with the commission. The commissioners and their staff are experienced, well

qualified, well informed, and diligent. Don't patronize or berate them in meetings or in filings.

8. *Coordinate FERC and Congressional strategy.* No agency can afford to ignore the Congress. FERC chairs have had different degrees of success in managing Congressional relations. A well-placed intervention from a well-informed legislator has its place. Threatening the FERC with pressure from Congress is counterproductive. Where a company supports a controversial FERC policy that has drawn fire from Capitol Hill, it is useful to support the FERC in the debate.

9. *Don't be afraid to go to court.* Judicial review has drawbacks. (i) It is expensive. (ii) It is protracted. In the two years it takes to get judicial review, the harm that has led the client to sue may already have been imposed, thus mooting the purpose of the challenge. (iii) Under deferential standards of judicial review, the commission starts off with an edge. One cannot count on overturning a commission ruling on appeal. At the same time, it is sometimes necessary to challenge the commission in court. Ideally with allies, judicial review at the right time on the right issue is important not only to try to reverse an unfavorable ruling, but also to show the commission that the company is not reluctant to appeal to the courts in appropriate cases.

Adding Value for the Client

I am fortunate to have divided my energy regulatory career over three decades between regulatory proceedings and court litigation. Experience with judicial review before the D.C. Circuit and other courts enables me to counsel clients to build a record before the FERC that will be useful on appeal.

Antitrust competence is an area of increasing importance that is often neglected by energy practitioners with too narrow a focus. In the past, state regulation of utilities was so extensive that under the "state action" doctrine, it was next to impossible to successfully challenge utility decisions under the antitrust laws. With the emergence of competition, the antitrust laws are becoming of increased significance.

We try to engage the Bureau of Competition staff at the Federal Trade Commission on issues where it may make sense for federal anti-trust regulators to weigh in. As the FERC considers its merger approval guidelines, or how to address transmission constraints, it is helpful to enlist the contribution of anti-trust regulators who have the most extensive experience in applying the Herfindahl-Hirschman merger review screens and other tools that can be used to assess market power.

It is very important to stay current in the energy area. This is not a field where a novice practitioner can look up black letter law in a treatise. Every day, one needs to check the commission Web site to read the decisions, as FERC policy, especially in light of the Energy Policy Act of 2005, is rapidly changing.

Staying current is more than a matter of reading FERC decisions: it is very important to review the daily filings. Review of daily filings is essential so that clients file timely interventions with substantive comments before the comment period closes (in some proceedings, fifteen days, in others, several weeks). We sometimes counsel intervention in a proceeding involving a utility or a region of the country where our clients would appear to have little direct interest simply because of precedential importance. Review of current filings also keeps one informed, as the state of the art changes with respect to market power analyses, analysis of conditions for regulatory approvals, and so on.

Changes in Energy Regulation

After years of consideration, in 2005 Congress enacted omnibus energy legislation, the Energy Policy Act of 2005. Since enactment, the FERC has undertaken a number of regulatory changes to implement the new statute. During this period of significant change, it has been important for energy lawyers to (i) make sure transactions faithfully apply the FERC's new approval process; (ii) watch for FERC proceedings in which clients should participate to protect their interests, whether to support or oppose FERC proposals or to bring the FERC's attention to real-world circumstances that warrant different or additional relief; and (iii) identify changes in energy markets that may represent new opportunities for clients.

WINNING STRATEGIES BEFORE THE FERC

For transactions, the most significant change is the repeal of the Public Utility Holding Company Act of 1935, which has severely restricted ownership of and investment in electric and natural gas utility companies and their corporate parents. Under the outmoded Public Utility Holding Company Act of 1935, acquisition of electric and natural gas utility interests in excess of a 10 percent threshold triggered onerous supervision and stringent oversight and other requirements administered by the Securities and Exchange Commission. With limited exceptions—most prominently, wholesale generation—companies not primarily engaged in utility operations could not acquire utilities with transmission and distribution systems or gas retail utilities, as the Public Utility Holding Company Act limited holding companies to operating utilities within a single integrated system. The Public Utility Holding Company Act obstacles also deterred foreign companies seeking to acquire U.S. utility interests.

Under the new regime, the full range of companies and institutions—including foreign investors, non-utility businesses, and financial institutions—are now able to acquire a broad spectrum of electricity and gas utility interests, and utilities will be able to merge without geographic restrictions. In lieu of regulation and oversight by the Securities and Exchange Commission, the FERC (as well as federal anti-trust authorities and, in the case of retail utilities, state commissions) will continue to pass on such acquisitions. Although the legislation modestly expanded the FERC's authority, its procedures and approval criteria are far less formidable and do not impose the roadblock that PUCHA represented. This opportunity for new entrants into U.S. electricity markets expands the potential base of clients calling upon the services of energy regulatory lawyers.

While many formerly barred transactions may now proceed, FERC approval is a prerequisite. The Energy Policy Act of 2005 modestly revises the FERC's merger authority to raise the threshold for FERC review of transactions to $10 million (with the exception of utility mergers, where there is no threshold) and grants the FERC jurisdiction over generation-only utilities. More significantly, the legislation grants the FERC new authority over certain transactions by "holding companies" with an electric utility or transmitting utility subsidiary. The statute and the FERC's implementing regulations establish a number of important exemptions from

59

these requirements. Nonetheless, as subject holding companies include those that directly or indirectly hold 10 percent or more of the voting securities of a public utility, many companies not traditionally identified as energy companies will now have transactions subject to FERC review. In conducting such reviews, the FERC is to determine whether the proposed transaction is in the public interest, with particular focus on whether any cross-subsidization of a non-utility associate company or pledge or encumbrance of utility assets for the benefit of an associate company would result. It is important for energy regulatory lawyers to inform their corporate colleagues about these new requirements and to ensure that the time and resources are allotted to address them in subject transactions.

As *quid pro quo* for repeal of the Public Utility Holding Company Act of 1935, the Energy Policy Act of 2005 seeks to deter any potential for abuse by granting the FERC authority to regulate and obtain access to the books and records of holding companies and related corporate entities. Although the FERC already has substantial books and records authorities under the Federal Power Act and Natural Gas Act, the new provisions may impose additional requirements, particularly on sibling and other entities that are not themselves utilities but are in the same corporate family as a utility. In particular, holding companies and their subsidiaries would have to maintain and make available "books, accounts, memoranda, and other records as [the FERC] determines are relevant to costs incurred…and necessary or appropriate for the protection of utility customers with respect to jurisdictional rates," and affiliate companies would have to maintain and make available all such documents relating to transactions with other affiliates. Under certain conditions, state utility commissions also may access such information. Various exemptions issued by the FERC, as well as the statutory limitation on the FERC's authority to those books and records "necessary or appropriate for the protection of utility customers," may avoid onerous application of the new requirements. The energy lawyer should assist potentially subject clients in understanding these requirements and in the filings that are necessary to notify the FERC of holding company status and the applicability of an exemption.

Many of the other important changes in the Energy Policy Act of 2005 address transmission issues, with widespread implications not only for transmission providers, but also for generators and end users. To ensure reliability and reduce the cost of delivered power to consumers by reducing transmission congestion, the act directs the FERC to establish incentive-based and performance-based rate treatments for interstate transmission of electric power by August of 2006. This provision aims to encourage economic efficiency and investment in the transmission grid by ensuring recovery of the investment in transmission rates. Because of the difficulty of recovering investment costs, investment in transmission facilities has lagged behind demand for use of those facilities over the past several years. With new regulations that will promote capital investment in expansion, improvement, maintenance, and operation of transmission facilities, provide a return on equity that attracts new investment, and encourage the deployment of transmission technologies that increase capacity and efficiency of existing facilities, such investment opportunities should appear more attractive and result in much-needed upgrades to improve and maintain system reliability.

The Energy Policy Act of 2005 extends open access to transmission services. To implement the new statutory directive on open access, the FERC is considering further remedies to address undue discrimination; reforms to the commission's pricing policies; changes to various services required under Order 888; possible penalties for violation of tariff provisions; and whether and how to reform its Open Access Transmission Tariff to reflect changes in the electric utility industry over the past decade. The revised rules should allow more participants into the markets throughout the country. While generators and transmission customers are the immediate beneficiaries, requiring all to play by the same rules ultimately will lead to improved transparency and hence improved competition throughout the system.

The Energy Policy Act of 2005 establishes new requirements for the FERC to address grid reliability, including certification of a new ERO. The ERO will develop mandatory reliability standards subject to FERC approval, and would have the ability to enforce the standards and impose reasonable penalties for violations by users or grid owners and operators. The ERO may also delegate enforcement authority to certain regional entities, provided they are governed by an independent board or a board that is adequately representative of stakeholders. Establishment of clear and uniform reliability standards has the potential to enhance opportunities for new investment in electricity transmission, provided that the FERC reasonably interprets and applies its new mandates.

The Energy Policy Act of 2005's implications are more mixed for qualifying cogeneration and small power production facilities (QFs). A QF is a generating facility that produces electricity and another form of useful thermal energy (such as heat or steam) primarily for industrial, commercial, heating, or cooling purposes. The Energy Policy Act of 2005 repeals the prior ownership restriction on QF ownership by electric utilities. With the lifting of this limitation, a facility may qualify as a QF even if it is 100 percent owned by a utility or affiliate, and there may be a number of utility acquisitions of ownership interests in QFs and increased trading of QF interests. But under certain circumstances, the Energy Policy Act of 2005 will nullify utilities' obligations to purchase power from QFs, which was the most important advantage of QF status. Although existing contracts with QFs are grandfathered, utilities will not be required to enter new contracts and may apply for relief from the obligation under the Public Utility Regulatory Policies Act of 1978 to purchase from and/or sell power to QFs where the FERC finds that a market is competitive and affords the QF non-discriminatory access to transmission and meaningful opportunities to engage in long- and short-term sales.

On the whole, however, the Energy Policy Act of 2005's sweeping changes to the existing electric regulatory regime eliminate many of the regulatory obstacles that have previously discouraged potential investors and increasing transparency. Energy regulatory lawyers have many new challenges and opportunities to bring these developments to the attention of companies that may not previously have contemplated investment in U.S. utilities.

Sara Schotland is a partner based in the Washington, D.C., office. She practices in the energy regulatory and litigation area. Mrs. Schotland joined the firm in 1972 and became a partner in 1980. She received a J.D. degree from Georgetown University Law Center in 1971 and an undergraduate degree, magna cum laude, from Harvard University in 1968. She clerked for the late Oscar Davis of the U.S. Court of Appeals for the Federal Circuit from 1971 to 1972. Mrs. Schotland is a member of the Bar in the District of

Columbia. She has been admitted to practice before numerous U.S. courts of appeal and district courts.

Mrs. Schotland has been practicing energy regulatory law since the 1970s. Since 1986, she has represented clients before the Federal Energy Regulatory Commission in the major Federal Energy Regulatory Commission restructuring proceedings, including proceedings related to formation of regional transmission organizations, mergers, market power analysis, open access transmission and transmission congestion, and capacity payments. Her clients include leading industrial consumers and independent generators of power such as ELCON and the American Iron and Steel Institute, power marketers including financial institutions such as JPMorgan, Bank of America, Barclays, and CSFB, and private equity firms engaged in energy transactions.

Mrs. Schotland regularly meets with Federal Energy Regulatory Commission commissioners and senior staff to discuss pending regulatory initiatives. She has also written and lectured on energy regulatory topics.

She has been involved in court cases relating to electricity deregulation, including representation of amicus Industrial Consumers in New York v. FERC, a U.S. Supreme Court case affirming the authority of Federal Energy Regulatory Commission jurisdiction over interstate transmission. She represented ELCON in a D.C. Circuit challenge to a Federal Energy Regulatory Commission decision approving the New York ISO demand curve methodology for measuring installed capacity payments.

Global Warming and the Coming Regulation of CO_2 Emissions

Philip L. Comella

Partner

Seyfarth Shaw LLP

Environmental laws historically begin with a catastrophe. In 1948, the inhabitants of Donora, Pennsylvania, experienced an air pollution disaster: smoke combined with a rare temperature inversion caused 7,000 illnesses and twenty deaths in a town of 14,000 people. Eight years later, Congress passed the first substantial air pollution control law. In the late 1960s, researchers at the California Institute of Technology isolated the source of the gray clouds that persistently blanketed Los Angeles; they found that hydrocarbons and nitrogen oxides from auto exhaust fumes produced the unwanted smog. In 1970, Congress passed the Clean Air Act Amendments and directed a new agency—the Environmental Protection Agency (EPA)—to implement it. In 1990, Congress substantially amended the Clean Air Act and implemented a new nationwide permitting system, controls on air toxics, and programs to reduce urban smog and acid rain.

In the late 1960s, the oil tanker *Torrey Canyon* collapsed off the southern coast of England, the tanker *Ocean Eagle* tore open near the coast of Puerto Rico, and an offshore oil rig exploded near Santa Barbara. Around the same time, industrial pollution caused Cleveland's Cuyahoga River to catch fire and poison fish that soon littered the beaches of Lake Erie. In 1970, Congress passed the Federal Water Pollution Control Act, under which the EPA seeks to maintain and improve water quality by limiting discharges to navigable waters.

For decades prior to 1980, many American companies disposed of hazardous substances along with their garbage, and usually in full compliance with state and federal laws. Episodes like the leaking waste ponds at Love Canal and the PCB-contaminated soil at Times Beach, however, soon made the federal government aware that existing solid waste disposal practices did not protect against the risks posed by hazardous wastes. Out of these disposal nightmares arose the Comprehensive Environmental Response, Compensation, and Liability Act of 1980 ("Superfund") and the Resource Conservation and Recovery Act. The Comprehensive Environmental Response, Compensation, and Liability Act of 1980 uses the dual threats of treble damages and escalating liability to force companies that contributed to historic pollution sites to pay clean-up costs, regardless of fault.

GLOBAL WARMING AND THE COMING REGULATION OF CO_2 EMISSIONS

In 1984, a Union Carbide plant in Bhopal, India, released a cloud of methyl isocyanate, killing 2,000 people and injuring thousands more. This event, and a similar though non-fatal one in West Virginia shortly thereafter, intensified the public's desire to know about the toxic chemicals industries emit into the environment. State and federal "right-to-know" laws quickly followed, led by Title III of the Superfund Amendments and Reauthorization Act, also known as the Emergency Planning and Community Right-to-Know Act of 1986. Title III requires thousands of industrial facilities to report annually on the amounts of toxic chemicals released into the environment, and it establishes a comprehensive notification and emergency response system in the event of a toxic release.

Will a Disaster Be Required?

The question is whether, in the coming decade, stronger hurricanes, melting glaciers, dwindling rain forests, spreading wildfires, drought, or other predicted environmental consequences will lead the United States to compel energy companies to reduce carbon dioxide emissions—the consensus cause of global warming.

The passage of environmental laws is a reaction to an associated disaster. But history shows that the emergency must be spectacular and attention-grabbing, and it must trigger severe environmental damage and health risks that no one can reasonably question. The Cuyahoga River burned; the Bhopal release killed thousands of people; Love Canal threatened the health of newborn babies. Will U.S. lawmakers require a disaster before taking action to regulate CO_2 emissions? No doubt exists that Hurricane Katrina focused the nation's attention like never before on the possible effect of global warming on natural disasters. But it looks like it will take more.

What Is Global Warming?

The term "global warming" refers to the increase in the Earth's temperature caused by human sources. A natural blanket of atmospheric gases insulates the Earth. These natural greenhouse gases—chiefly water vapor, carbon dioxide, ozone, nitrous oxide, and methane—allow the penetration of sunlight that warms the Earth; the light rays then reflect off the Earth's surface and head back to space. On the return trip, the insulating blanket captures a portion of the reflecting radiation and traps it near the Earth's surface, providing a climate fit for life. Without the insulating effect of the natural greenhouse, the Earth's temperature would be about 90 degrees colder. The natural greenhouse balances the Earth's climate to allow life to thrive.

Comparisons with the atmospheres of the Earth's closest neighboring planets, Mars and Venus, are often used to illustrate this point. The atmosphere of Mars, for example, is extremely thin and consequently traps little heat, making the average surface temperature of Mars about −50 degrees C. In contrast, the atmosphere of Venus consists of about 95 percent CO_2, creating dense insulation and resulting in surface temperatures of +460 degrees C.

Carbon Dioxide and Global Warming

The consensus in the scientific community is that human-generated greenhouse gases, particularly carbon dioxide, have altered the composition of the natural insulation and thereby unnaturally warmed the Earth. Although climate dynamics are notoriously complex, two data points are most telling—CO_2 concentrations in the atmosphere and average global temperatures.

Prior to the industrial revolution in the 1800s, the atmospheric concentration of CO_2 ranged from about 190 parts per million (ppm) to 280 ppm. By 1958, the CO_2 concentration had risen to 315 ppm, and by the year 2000, 370 ppm. Recent calculations show the number approaching 400 ppm; by 2050, the concentration is expected to reach 500 ppm without changes in CO_2 emission rates. (*Scientific American*, September 2006)

An increase in the average surface temperature of the Earth roughly correlates with the rise in CO_2 emissions. Prior to 1900, the average global surface temperature was about 13.7 degrees C. A recent lengthy study by the Intergovernmental Panel on Climate Change reports that the average global temperature increased by about 0.6 degrees C during the twentieth century and that if the present trend continues, temperatures will rise between 1.4 and 5.8 degrees C by the end of the century. Virtually all of the twenty warmest years recorded occurred since 1980, with 2005 being the warmest year ever recorded.

The relatively sharp increase in temperatures beginning in the last two decades of the twentieth century accounts for the controversial "hockey-stick" graph, first drawn by the Intergovernmental Panel on Climate Change. Studies conducted by the National Research Council have recently supported this increase in temperatures. Thus, global warming appears to correlate with the increasing concentration of human-generated CO_2 found in the atmosphere.

The two major sources of the increase in global warming are the burning of fossil fuels (i.e., coal, oil, and natural gas) and deforestation in tropical climates. Fossil fuel burning adds to the amount of CO_2; deforestation reduces a major source to absorb the CO_2 emitted. Fossil fuel combustion accounts for almost all of the human-generated CO_2 in the United States, amounting to roughly 5,725 million metric tons (or teragrams) in 2000, which is estimated to rise to roughly 7,655 million metric tons by 2020.

Does Global Warming Cause Stronger Hurricanes?

This question was the top science story of 2005 according to *Discover* magazine. Tropical ocean waters power hurricanes. The warmer the water, the greater the evaporation rate; as the evaporating water cools, it releases energy, leading to stronger hurricanes. That is the theory. Recent studies conducted by researches from MIT, the Georgia Institute of Technology, and the National Center for Atmospheric Research have found that although the number of hurricanes has not increase over the past several decades, their ferocity has. Other researches question the correlation between global warming and hurricane strength, attributing the string of powerful 2005 hurricanes, Katrina, Rita, and Wilma among them, to natural climate fluctuations. A reduction in hurricanes or hurricane strength may cast doubt on the global-warming connection. But every variation in hurricane pattern over the next several years is likely to re-focus attention on the possibility that indeed, global warming has something to do with it.

Levels of Certainty

Wrapped within the global warming debate is the level of certainty required before the government should take action. A recent report prepared by the National Research Council concluded that a causal link between greenhouse gas emissions and global warming "cannot be unequivocally established." At the same time, an article in a recent issue of *Scientific American* concludes that the debate of whether CO_2 emissions cause global warming is over—scientists have established the link. But as a dissenting opinion in the leading global warming case of *Commonwealth of Massachusetts v. Environmental Protection Agency*, 415 F.3d 50 (D.C. Cir. 2005), *cert. granted*, 125 S. Ct. 2960 (2006), observes, environmental regulation does not require mathematical certainty. The Clean Air Act, like environmental laws in general, are based on reasonably possible risks. The Clean Air Act in particular requires the EPA to regulate pollutants that may "reasonably be anticipated to endanger" human welfare. Overbreadth is one of the hallmarks of environmental regulation. Allowable concentrations of hazardous substances in the soil, groundwater, or drinking water are usually pegged well below the actual health-based levels, and the medical connection between many substances, such as PCBs and human illness, is often uncertain.

In a civil courtroom, the plaintiff does not have to prove his or her case with scientific or mathematical certainty; rather, he or she need only show that it is more likely than not the defendant caused the harm. Expert witnesses testify to a "reasonable degree" of scientific certainty, not absolute certainty.

Can the U.S. Legal System Handle the Enormity of this Problem?

The effort is already underway to use the legal system to regulate CO_2 emissions. But more so than any environmental emergency yet encountered, global warming presents daunting challenges to the legal system.

In *State of Connecticut v. American Electric Power*, 406 F. Supp. 2d 265 (S.D. N.Y. 2005), a group of states, representing 77 million people, brought a public nuisance action against a number of electric power producers for emitting the carbon dioxide that causes global warming. Despite the flurry of statistics linking the defendants' fossil fuel burning activities to the onset of global warming, the court dismissed the complaint because it raised a non-justiciable political question, not a legal one. Congress, the court said, was the appropriate branch of government to address the intricate policy question of global warming.

In the wake of Hurricane Katrina, and the possible association with global warming, a number of lawsuits were filed against oil and chemical companies for their alleged role in producing the emissions that led to global warming, and by some extremely attenuated line of reasoning led to Hurricane Katrina. *See Cox v. Nationwide Mutual Insurance Company*, Case No. 1:05CV436 LG-RHW (U.S. District Court, S.D. Miss.) This complaint alleges that:

> The Oil Company Defendant Class has engaged in activities that have produced the greatest single source of by-products leading to the development and increase of global warming.
>
> * * *
>
> As a direct and proximate result of the activities of the Oil Company Defendant Class and the environmentally harmful by-products produced thereby, there has been a marked increase in global warming which, in turn, produced the conditions whereby a storm of the strength and size of Hurricane Katrina would inevitably form and strike the Mississippi Gulf Coast consequently causing extensive death and destruction.

Although not directly ruling on the merits of these claims, the Mississippi court had this to say about the global warming claim:

> I will observe that there exists a sharp difference of opinion in the scientific community concerning the causes of global warming, and I foresee daunting evidentiary problems for anyone who undertakes to prove, by a preponderance of the evidence, the degree to which the actions of any individual oil company, any individual

chemical company, or the collective action of these corporations contribute, through the emission of greenhouse gases, to global warming; and the extent to which the emission of greenhouse gases by these defendants, through the phenomenon of global warming, intensified or otherwise affected the weather system that produced Hurricane Katrina. This is a task that the plaintiffs are free to undertake if that is their intention, and I am confident that due consideration will be given to the requirements Rule 11, F.R. Civ. P.

Comer v. Nationwide Mutual Insur. Co., 2006 WL 1066645 (S.D. Miss.) Rule 11 requires litigants to have a good faith basis for asserting any claim or defense; lawyers who cannot demonstrate such a good faith basis are subject to sanctions.

These two decisions, though likely the first of many to come, highlight the daunting challenge parties will face when attempting to use the common law tort system to change conduct in the area of global warming. A core problem is the issue of causation, or in legal terms, proximate cause. Although the concept of proximate cause admits of no single definition and is among the most debated concepts in tort law, it generally consists of two elements: the "but for" test and foreseeability, substantiality, or other policy judgment that restricts the overly inclusive reach of the "but for" test.

The "but for" test means what it says: an event is considered the cause of another event if, but for the first event, the second would not have occurred. Thus, but for the speeding car, the collision with the stopped bus would not have occurred; or but for the pass interference by a defensive back in football, the receiver would have caught the ball. In each example, the effect would not have occurred but for the triggering event.

Simply using the "but for" test as a standard of legal liability, however, is prone to abuse. As one goes back into the chain of events, he or she reaches causes that are so remote in time or place that ascribing fault would be wrong as a matter of social policy. For example, one can trace the cause for the speeding car's being on the road to the car manufacturer that increased the horsepower from the prior year, the salesperson who sold the car, the high school driving instructor, and so on. Inherent in the legal concept of proximate cause is a policy judgment concerning who, if anyone, should be responsible for an accident.

On the other hand, if a supposed cause fails the "but for" test, the case is closed, and this is the problem with using the tort system for attributing fault to emitters of CO_2. Plaintiffs must show that an energy producer's (or group of producers) emissions caused global warming, and then deal with the intractable follow-up conundrum of showing how the emissions led to the harm they complain of.

With approximately 6,500 million metric tons of CO_2 currently emitted by all U.S. sources, blaming one company or group of companies for global warming will undoubtedly fail the "but for" test. The causal link becomes even more speculative when a specific defendant or group of defendants is blamed for causing an environmental disaster linked with global warming, such as stronger hurricanes. If CO_2 emissions indeed cause global warming and if global warming leads to stronger hurricanes (the number-one science story in 2005, according to *Discover Magazine*, was "Does Global Warming Make Hurricanes Worse?"), then it would be the joint activity of millions of CO_2 emitters that caused the problem. No single drop in the bucket caused it to overflow.

Superfund Squared

To place liability upon contributors to global warming would require a new causation scheme. It would make a CO_2 emitter liable for the sheer act of contributing to the problem. Liability would have to be strict, with no defenses, including the defense that the emissions were permitted, lawful, or necessary. Liability would have to be joint and several, making the emitter liable for the entire harm, unless it could distinguish its contribution from others. The new scheme would have to revise the common law tort system to make the "polluter" strictly liable for the resulting harm.

Despite the radical features of such a law, there is already established precedent in environmental law for such a draconian liability scheme: the law is Superfund, or the Comprehensive Environmental Response, Compensation, and Liability Act.

Superfund was intended to make up for the historical absence of rules governing the proper disposal of hazardous substances on the land. Congress, in passing this law, was faced with hundreds of abandoned hazardous waste sites, many of which were leading to serious contamination of groundwater and surface water, with no viable owner or operator or financial assurance to clean up the problem. To address this state of affairs, Congress took radical action. Superfund imposes strict liability upon any party that generated waste found at the contaminated site, irrespective of whether the generator selected the site, was aware of it, or whether the particular waste caused the environmental problems. The EPA need not prove that your waste caused the contamination; it need only show that waste like yours was found at the site. *U.S. v. Monsanto Co.*, 858 F.2d 160 (4th Cir. 1988), *cert. denied*, 490 U.S. 1106 (1989). Unless it can prove that the harm at the site is divisible, a potentially responsible party may be liable for the entire cost of clean-up. *See U.S. v. Alcan Aluminum Corp.*, 990 F.2d 711 (2d Cir. 1993); *U.S. v. Chem-Dyne*, 572 F. Supp. 802 (S.D. Ohio 1983).

But it took the front-page horrors of Love Canal, Times Beach, Valley of the Drums, and many other hazardous waste crises to motivate lawmakers to transform thousands of formerly law-abiding corporations into potentially responsible parties. Superfund has cost businesses billions of dollars in clean-up costs to remedy environmental problems they did not necessarily cause. It transformed the concept of fault from the common law tort principle, where a defendant's act must cause the harm, to making the mere act of generating a hazardous waste a culpable activity.

Superfund may be a blueprint for a global warming liability scheme, as similarities exist. This new, enhanced Superfund would base liability for the consequences of global warming upon the mere emission of greenhouse gases. CO_2 emitters would be strictly liable for having contributed to global warming irrespective of whether their own "drop in the bucket" caused the harm. But now, instead of digging up buried drums of hazardous waste and pump-and-treating groundwater, responsible parties would be funding global warming studies, experimenting with new technologies, re-foresting barren areas, meeting renewable energy requirements, sequestering carbon, and undertaking a host of activities that current law allows but does not compel.

Can the global warming version of Superfund be passed? It seems unlikely now, but given a global warming catastrophe of enough magnitude, it is not out of the realm of possibility.

Important Clean Air Act Developments

The most significant global warming case brought to date is now pending in the U.S. Supreme Court. In this case, *Commonwealth of Massachusetts v. Environmental Protection Agency*, 415 F. 3d 50 (D.C. Cir. 2005), *cert. granted*, 126 S. Ct. 2960 (2006), a divided panel of the U.S. Court of Appeals for the D.C. Circuit denied a petition filed by twelve states, three cities, an American territory, and numerous environmental organizations to compel the EPA to regulate CO_2 emissions from motor vehicles. The EPA denied the rule-making on several grounds, including the scientific uncertainty about the consequences of greenhouse gas emissions on future climate conditions, the lack of specific Congressional statutory direction on global warming, its agency discretion, and the EPA's position that carbon dioxide is not a "pollutant" under the Clean Air Act. The petitioners then filed suit in the D.C. Circuit to compel the EPA to undertake the rule-making.

Two of the three judges wrote opinions denying the petition for review, though on different grounds. In his dissenting opinion, Judge Tatel concluded that the EPA violated the following mandate in the Clean Air Act: "The Administrator shall by regulation prescribe...standards applicable to the emission of any air pollutant from...new motor vehicles...which in his judgment cause, or contribute to, air pollution which may reasonably be anticipated to endanger public health or welfare." The argument is that carbon dioxide, in the context of global warming, is a pollutant and the statute states that the EPA shall regulate pollutants. With respect to the scientific uncertainty issue, Judge Tatel, as noted above, pointed out that environmental regulation does not require scientific certainty; rather, when health and the environment are at risk, probable threats must also be addressed. Reviewing the technical submissions, including that of the National Research Council, he stated that he had "grave difficulty seeing how" the EPA...could possibly fail to conclude that global warming "may reasonably be anticipated to endanger public health or welfare." But this opinion is in dissent, and predicting the outcome of the U.S. Supreme Court opinion is itself an uncertain venture. Should the court get to the merits, however, and find that the EPA is obligated to regulate CO_2 as a pollutant, the regulatory climate will change dramatically.

Voluntary Programs

Voluntary compliance with a regulatory norm is always the preferred approach. It allows affected companies to better adapt their businesses to the environmental standard and focus resources on achieving the standard rather than on contesting enforcement. A number of voluntary programs are currently in place to reduce greenhouse-gas emissions, with the most prominent among them, the Chicago Climate Exchange (CCX). Members of the CCX commit to reducing their greenhouse gas emissions by a certain percentage every year. Those who do better than their commitment can sell the excess emission credits on the exchange or bank them for later use. Those that cannot meet their budget must buy available credits over the exchange. Supply and demand determines the price of the credits. The CCX, like similar programs, is based on the so-called cap-and-trade program established under the Clean Air Act for reducing sulfur dioxide emissions. The success of the CAA program has spurred interest in developing a similar program for CO2.

One notable difference between the CCX and the CAA SO2 program, however, is that the CAA set a legal cap on the total allowable SO2 emissions nationwide and then set up an emission trading program. The CCX and similar programs operate only with self-imposed, individual caps, and thus do not control total greenhouse-gas emissions. Non-participants may be increasing their emissions more than the total reductions agreed to by CCX members. As extensively publicized, the United States is not part of the international agreement for reducing greenhouse gases on a global basis known as the Kyoto Protocol. The U.S. did not sign on to the Kyoto Protocol chiefly because it could not reconcile its allotted reduction target of CO2 emissions (7% below 1990 levels) with its economic growth and it could not accept the exclusion of developing countries, such as China and Mexico, from being subject to any CO2 reduction. Despite the flaws in both voluntary emission-reduction programs and the Kyoto Protocol, carbon dioxide emission limits and trading will likely be part of any future regulatory program to address global warming.

Conclusion

Addressing the predicted environmental consequences from global warming presents a great challenge to lawmakers. Every U.S. citizen depends upon an ample and steady supply of energy and, as of today, fossil fuels produce the overwhelming proportion of that energy. With energy dependence comes CO_2 emissions and the increasingly certain impact on global warming. The question of environmental regulation has always involved competing social, economic, scientific, and political values. Global warming now stands at the convergence point of these competing values.

CO_2 regulation is coming. It may be in the form of statutory controls under the Clean Air Act, a global warming Superfund, or groundbreaking tort action. If the scientists are right, we will suffer a pivotal event, a disaster, that awakens the country to the importance of addressing the problem with all the force of the federal and state government. Acting sooner has the benefit of both preparing for the involuntary controls and perhaps doing a small part to delay—if not avoid—the day of reckoning.

Philip Comella is head of the environmental, safety, and toxic torts group in the Chicago office of Seyfarth Shaw LLP and a member of the Leading Lawyer network in environmental law. Mr. Comella has broad experience defending state and federal enforcement actions brought under a host of different environmental laws, including Superfund, RCRA, TSCA, the Clean Air Act, and the Clean Water Act. He has defended companies from toxic tort lawsuits in a variety of contexts relating to the release of hazardous chemicals, and he has extensive experience defending environmental and engineering professionals against negligence and contract claims. In the growing area of renewable energy, he has wide-ranging experience with environmental, contractual, and tax issues involving the use of landfill gas as an alternate energy source. He has addressed numerous environmental issues arising from real property transfers, including the adequacy of environmental assessments, potential claims against sellers for undisclosed contamination, and the use of voluntary clean-up ("Brownfield") programs. He lectures frequently on current topics in environmental law, including due diligence in mergers and acquisitions and hazardous waste.

Prior to joining Seyfarth Shaw, Mr. Comella spent seven years as in-house counsel for a major waste management company, where he had responsibility for hazardous waste issues arising across the country.

He earned his J.D., with honors, from George Washington University in 1983.

Practicing Clean Energy Law: A Focus on Solar

Daniel Yost
Partner
Lou Soto
Partner
Mitch Zuklie
Partner

Orrick, Herrington & Sutcliffe LLP

The Role of an Attorney in Clean Energy Law

As oil prices rise and concerns mount over the world's continued dependence on non-renewable energy sources, politicians, scientists, and investors alike are focusing more of their attention on a rapidly growing industry: "cleantech." The term cleantech refers to energy and energy-related technologies that provide environmentally friendly solutions to today's resource problems. Examples of cleantech include solar and wind power, as well as the use of biofuels such as ethanol. Research on clean technologies started more than twenty years ago, but it is only within the past several years that the market for clean energy has truly begun to soar.

The *Cleantech Venture Capital Report* states that between 1999 and 2005, venture capitalists invested more than $7.3 billion in North American cleantech companies, with approximately $4.9 billion from 2002 to 2005 alone. The report projects that investments will continue to rise; over the next three years, venture capital investments in cleantech will total between $6.2 and $8.8 billion. At the moment, solar power is the most mature segment of the industry, with three cleantech companies, Sunpower, Suntech Power, and Q-Cells, going public last year. These initial public offerings were three of the largest in 2005.

As an attorney, working on deals with cleantech companies requires a different skill set than working with an Internet or other traditional technology startup. Although there is some overlap, the differences in the industries necessitate an attorney or set of attorneys who are sensitive to the particular needs of cleantech companies. This chapter explores critical skills sets for attorneys dealing with cleantech companies in general, and solar companies in particular, focusing specifically on two of the three public solar companies, Sunpower and Suntech Power; also included are data about two private solar companies, Advent Solar and Nanosolar. While this chapter focuses on solar companies, ideally this comparison will be illustrative of the unique skills required of attorneys working in any of the cleantech fields generally.

Capital Requirements

Solar companies' capital requirements tend to be much larger than the requirements of startups in many other technology sectors. In their second rounds of financing in 2005, Nanosolar and Advent Solar raised $20 million and $30 million, respectively (source: www.venturesource.com). The *2006 Venture Capital Industry Report* reports that the median amount raised by any company in 2005 in a second-round financing was $8.0 million, and the median raised by any information technology company in any round of financing was $7.0 million. According to www.venturesource.com, in 2006 Nanosolar went on to close a round of financing at $75 million. These companies sought out such large investments because, like most solar companies, they required significant amounts of capital to operate. Solar companies have opportunities to diversify sources of funding, which can come from multiple private sources or in the form of government incentives, to meet capital needs.

Many solar companies incur very high operating costs because of the need to build a state-of-the-art manufacturing facility for the production of its solar products. Other contributing factors to the high operating costs include the money needed to purchase the expensive raw materials that form the basis of solar technologies and the expense of maintaining a staff of highly trained scientists dedicated to research, development, and preparing to solve the sorts of problems that arise when working with a new technology.

In many instances, the largest cost for an early-stage solar company is the creation of a manufacturing facility for its solar products. SunPower, for instance, just built a $330 million facility in the Philippines in 2004.

Although the money spent building these facilities would appear to be a one-time cost, both Sunpower and Suntech Power state that they will continue to spend large amounts of capital on operating and expanding their facilities. SunPower plans to spend approximately $100 million in 2006 to expand its manufacturing capacity and diversify its product offerings (source: SunPower prospectus dated May 31, 2006).

One of the largest costs associated with operating a solar business is the rising price of polysilicon, which is in gravely short supply and yet very high demand. Suntech Power states that it plans to spend $100 million of the proceeds from its initial public offering on raw materials, which include polysilicon (source: Suntech Power prospectus dated December 14, 2005). Given such prices and the limited supply of raw materials, solar cells must be as efficient as possible if they are to serve as a viable alternative to fossil fuels. Currently, most solar cells in commercial production have a conversion efficiency of about 15 percent, meaning they harness about 15 percent of the light energy that hits them. At some point, however, the Earth's supply of polysilicon will deplete, and if efficiencies remain this low, there will not be enough raw material to meet current energy demands. For these reasons, significant research and development money are placed into making the solar cells as efficient as possible. Suntech Power states that it will spend approximately $20 million of the funds raised in its initial public offering for the enhancement of research and development initiatives (source: Suntech Power Prospectus dated December 14, 2005). It will also dedicate a portion of these funds to researching other avenues for harnessing light energy so that less polysilicon is required to harvest more of the energy captured from the sunlight. SunPower manufactures cells with a conversion efficiency of 21 percent, making their cells more efficient than those of many other companies.

Government Incentives and Teaming Arrangements

In order to reduce the solar company's share of research and development costs, some solar companies are teaming up with national laboratories. SunPower participates in a cost-sharing research program with the National Renewable Energy Laboratory that offsets its research and development expenses by approximately $1 million a year and allows it to develop new technologies more rapidly (source: SunPower Prospectus dated May 31, 2006). Nanosolar and Advent Solar both licensed their technology that was developed at Sandia National Labs (source: www.venturesource.com).

One potential source of funding comes from government incentives. Because governments around the world are realizing that the world faces an energy crisis, local and national governments are subsidizing solar production through consumer incentives. China launched an aggressive national renewable energy policy in February of 2006 with a $3.5 billion plan that aims to boost solar production to 500MW by 2010. In January of 2006, California approved a $3 billion solar initiative that will be implemented over the next eleven years. These consumer incentive programs will serve to keep solar energy competitive with traditional energy sources and increase demand for solar energy in the coming years.

Project Finance

One possible source of funding is the "project finance" market that provides capital for many energy and infrastructure projects. Project finance generally is considered to be debt financing that is provided on the strength of the anticipated net cash flow of an entity established for the sole purpose of developing, constructing, owning/leasing, and operating a standalone business enterprise such as an electric generating facility. Because lenders will not be looking to the balance sheet of an established, creditworthy entity as security for repayment of the loan, the commercial and contractual arrangements that comprise the project, including the identity and creditworthiness of counterparties to key contracts, will serve as the real basis for the extension of credit. A solar business might use project financing to fund a manufacturing facility that had long-term agreements in place with purchasers of its products. Project financing can also be used in a "merchant" setting where products are sold into an established market rather than to specific buyers under long-term contracts. An example of this is what is being done for new ethanol projects. Most ethanol projects need up-front money to pay for construction and input costs (i.e., feedstock and steam), and the end product is sold into the ethanol energy market. However, this approach requires more equity than would be needed in a "fully contracted" deal; it works only where experts can issue a report concluding that market prices over the term of the debt will be sufficient to support debt service.

Non-recourse loans typically will be made only if a project's commercial and contractual arrangements can be expected to generate revenues predictably and reliably across a range of anticipated operating scenarios. These revenues must represent a multiple (usually an average of at least 1.5 to 1.00, and preferably much higher) of scheduled debt service after deducting all operation and maintenance expenses, including funding of reasonable reserves. Such arrangements necessarily must be in place for at least the scheduled term of the debt.

In order to benefit from a project's commercial and contractual arrangements following a borrower default, project finance lenders (or, in the case of foreclosure, purchasers) must be able to step into the borrower's shoes with respect to all of its various rights and obligations relating to the project, including real and personal property interests, permits and other governmental approvals, and contracts. Thus, in addition to being satisfied with the commercial basis of a deal, lenders must be assured of having enforceable security interests in everything necessary for the project to generate the required revenues.

Intellectual Property Issues

Several unique intellectual property issues surround cleantech companies. Many cleantech companies' technologies spun out of research that was conducted at university or government laboratories. Advent Solar and Nanosolar, for instance, started based on technologies developed at Sandia National Laboratories. Therefore, attorneys representing cleantech companies must understand how best to draft licensing agreements with government entities and universities that will be favorable to the company. Attorneys representing investors seeking to invest in cleantech companies also should have expertise with licensing agreements, so as to be able to advise investors on the terms and conditions applicable to those licenses governing the cleantech company's core intellectual property.

An issue of which counsel should be aware is "march-in" rights, which are generally present when a company uses U.S. government funding in the development of its product. March-in rights refer to the government's right to require the company with whom it works to grant a license to a responsible applicant; if the company refuses to comply, the government can grant the license itself. Such action would expose the company to the risk of disclosure of confidential information and intellectual property rights to third parties, including competitors. SunPower's agreement with the government is subject to such rights. Companies seeking to enter into relationships with the government or investors seeking to invest in companies that have already done so should consult with attorneys who understand the scope and limitations of such rights.

Traditional intellectual property issues arise in the solar industry, but with slight twists. Generally, solar companies rely on a combination of patent, trademark, and trade secret law to protect their intellectual property. Substantive knowledge in these areas of intellectual property law is therefore critical. Patent issues in cleantech may be subject to a host of landmines, as there is generally considerable prior art that needs to be considered when determining the scope of patent claims. Also, with several competing solar companies pursuing essentially the same goals, it is important to understand which types of technologies are patentable and which are not. Similarly, it is imperative that attorneys representing solar companies understand trade secret law in order to advise on the best practices that are used to prevent disclosure of highly proprietary confidential information. Trademark issues in the solar area are made more complicated by the production and sale of products in different countries that place solar companies in an international context. SunPower, for instance, was unable to obtain a trademark on its name in any country other than the United States. Because SunPower sells many of its products outside of the United States (66 percent in the three months ending on March 31, 2006, and 70 percent in 2005), such trademark issues could affect its selling potential in other countries, as other companies could dilute the mark or even trade on the goodwill of SunPower's name. Attorneys need to be aware of these issues and must be able to handle twists in traditional intellectual property law to effectively represent solar companies and investors who wish to invest in solar technology.

Government Regulations

Attorneys working with solar companies need to understand all government regulations applicable to energy companies. As SunPower and Suntech Power both point out in their prospecti, one of the major risk factors they face is that energy law might change, forcing them to alter the way they do business. Further complicating the issue is the fact that energy law differs from country to country and to some extent between states in the United States. Again, because these companies operate under the laws of many different countries, cleantech attorneys must understand the energy laws of different countries.

Adding Value to Clients: The Importance of Attorneys Working for Cleantech

Although there is some overlap in the skills required of attorneys working for a cleantech company with those who work with more traditional technology companies, the skill sets required to represent cleantech companies may ultimately be broader. This is due to the fact that cleantech requires investment of more capital than does a traditional startup company due to higher operating costs. These costs require a cleantech company to seek non-traditional sources of funding, and because of this, an attorney in this field must be both creative and well versed in the applicable laws and options available to clients. Secondly, with respect to cleantech law, intellectual property issues are more complex as a result of complicated licensing issues, as well the presence of government funding and international concerns. Finally, the body of energy laws governing cleantech companies is substantially different from those governing other industries. For these reasons, an experienced attorney who works for cleantech companies will be better able to navigate the complex and fluctuating laws facing those in this industry and will be comfortable and innovative with respect to advising on non-traditional sources of funding.

Daniel Yost, *a partner in Orrick's Silicon Valley office, is a member of the corporate group. Mr. Yost's practice focuses on negotiating complex commercial and technology transactions and intellectual property counseling.*

Mr. Yost has counseled clients on commercial law, copyright, licensing, marketing, patent, privacy, strategic alliances, trademark, and trade secret matters. Mr. Yost has represented companies in various industries including: biotechnology, consumer electronics, energy, hardware, Internet, media, semiconductor, services, software, telecommunications, and wireless.

Mr. Yost received his J.D. from the University of California at Berkeley's Boalt Hall School of Law. During law school, he completed internships with the fraud investigation unit of the U.S. Securities and Exchange Commission and the Honorable William Schwarzer of the Northern District of California.

He was a Fulbright Scholar at Oxford University. He received his B.A. from the University of California at Santa Cruz with highest honors in economics and honors in American studies.

Lou Soto, *a partner in the firm's Silicon Valley office, is a member of Orrick's emerging companies group, which advises emerging companies, public companies, venture capital firms, and investment banks.*

Mr. Soto focuses his practice on emerging growth companies in the technology and life science sectors. He frequently represents companies in venture financing, public offering, corporate partnership, and acquisition transactions as well as in corporate governance, securities counseling, and general corporate matters.

Mr. Soto also has extensive experience representing venture capital funds such as Montreux Equity Partners, Maveron, ZG Capital, and C2C Ventures.

Mr. Soto is a founding member of the firm's corporate practice in Silicon Valley.

Mitchell Zuklie, *a partner in the firm's Silicon Valley office, is a member of Orrick's emerging companies group, which advises emerging companies, public companies, venture capital firms, and investment banks. Mr. Zuklie focuses on the formation, financing, and general corporate counseling of technology businesses. He has completed several hundred venture capital financings, and numerous public offerings, mergers, acquisitions, and technology licensing transactions.*

Mr. Zuklie has represented numerous venture capital clients including Accel Partners, Benchmark Capital, Bessemer Venture Partners, Mohr, Davidow Ventures, U.S. Venture Partners, and Sequoia Capital. He has also represented investment banks including Goldman, Sachs & Co., and Credit Suisse First Boston.

Mr. Zuklie serves as a director of the California Law Review, *and was one of the authors of the National Venture Capital Association's model venture capital financing forms.*

Before joining Orrick, Mr. Zuklie was a director at Venture Law Group.

Christian Sjulsen, *also of Orrick, Herrington and Sutcliffe LLP's Silicon Valley office, assisted with the writing of this chapter. Mr. Sjulsen is a law student at Stanford Law School, where he expects to receive his J.D. in 2008. Mr. Sjulsen has a B.A. in chemistry from Columbia University.*

Acknowledgment: *Thanks to Keith Kriebel of Orrick's Washington, D.C., office for his valuable insights on project finance.*

Protecting an Energy Company's Intellectual Property

Charles E. Frost Jr.
Shareholder – Intellectual Property, Oil & Gas, and Commercial Litigation
Chamberlain, Hrdlicka, White, Williams & Martin

Introduction

As the world of business becomes more focused on intellectual property and communication, the challenges—and the stakes—are changing. The more we communicate, the greater the opportunities for miscommunication—and the worse the possible ramifications. This chapter will address two specific problems that are endemic in the energy business: (1) the risk that disputes cannot be fairly and cost-efficiently resolved because of exploding e-mail and the related problems created in electronic discovery, and (2) protecting companies' intellectual property.

E-Mail and Electronic Discovery

It is a fact of life that there will be disputes both among companies and between companies and individuals. Such disputes are dealt with in our society through the litigation and courtroom process, called arbitration.

E-mails and discovery of e-mail, and attached documents, in litigation is becoming a huge problem. More than 85 percent of information today never reaches the paper stage. Vast volumes of information are stored on computers. Many communications are exchanged by e-mail daily. This results in a huge proliferation of data. E-mails within companies, and inter-company, spawn huge volumes of lengthy e-mails, with the original e-mail stacked on top of the second e-mail, stacked on top of the third e-mail, and so on, often with documents attached.

There are no standards on how documents are stored. A single company may use a number of different methods of storing documents. Data also frequently is stored in diverse formats and programs, making it harder to examine. To compound the challenges, with modern Blackberries, PDAs, and similar devices, and with the advent of instant messaging and blogging, and now "unified messaging," companies face major challenges with controlling the generation of, and producing, electronic data.

The challenge of locating all the various places data is stored, and the added challenge of even having the requisite outdated software to access, print, and use old stored information is at least frustrating, and sometimes impossible to resolve. For example, if the dispute requires access to and production of data more than four years old, the computer program to access that data may no longer be available. Likewise, if officers and employees of the company are using a variety of information tools, from desktop computers to Blackberries to cell phones with information systems, and if all of the information is not fed back into a centralized system, all of those various sources must be accessed to meet a request for production from the opposing party when a dispute arises. This can be exacerbated by turnover of personnel.

E-mails and documents attached to them must be reviewed by attorneys familiar with the case, because there is a danger of producing information beyond the scope of the request and/or disclosing personal, privileged information (which could be a violation of state or federal law) or producing attorney/client-privileged information. Some new computer programs help in the culling process, but it is still an arduous and expensive task. (I have been made aware last week of a new program that may be available soon that the inventors hope will substantially reduce the costs, but it is unproven at this time.) Indeed, the cost of producing, and of lawyers reviewing, such huge e-mail chains is making dispute resolution so expensive that in many cases it is becoming prohibitive—resulting in disputes being settled for the wrong reasons.

On top of all the foregoing, there also is a danger of losing electronic documents. Litigation lawyers frequently hope to find that documents have been "lost" or destroyed by the opposing party so they can build a case for "spoliation." If they are successful in building a spoliation case, they try to get the judge to instruct the jury to consider the missing documents as evidence against the party that lost or destroyed them. Such an instruction could change the entire flavor of the case, and the case once again may be resolved unfavorably for the wrong reasons.

Frequently, people take far too casual an attitude concerning e-mail within companies. Engineers, project managers, accountants, and others focus on accomplishing their jobs and usually have little or no understanding of the risk to their companies and, concomitantly, their own futures from casual and undisciplined spawning of e-mail. It is not enjoyable to have to rein in the rampant abuse of e-mail, but it could easily make the difference between being able to engage in cost-effective dispute resolution (whether

91

arbitration or litigation) versus having to simply give up on a legitimate claim or defense because of the cost of managing the e-mail discovery.

In addition, employees frequently are far too casual with what they put in e-mails. An e-mail should be treated exactly like a "snail mail" letter. That is, before an e-mail is sent, it should be printed out and edited just as with a regular letter. This includes thinking, "What would this look like in a courtroom two years from now?" (I print out virtually all of my e-mail and edit them before sending them; when I don't, I frequently regret having failed to do so.)

An example of the care that must be taken with e-mails was provided in a recent article in the *Wall Street Journal*. A young intern at a large company sent an e-mail to his friends—and forty employees, including some decision-makers, at his place of summer employment—stating, "I'm busy doing [nothing]. Went to a nice 2hr sushi lunch today at Sushi Zen. Nice place. Spent the rest of the day typing e-mails and [gabbing] with people." For a horror story of energy company corporate e-mails, see www.enronemail.com, which contains over 500,000 e-mails sent by Enron employees during the last few months of the company.

A related problem is retaining documents, including e-mail, for adequate periods of time. Many federal and state statutes, regulations, and agency rules impose mandatory retention periods on certain types of documents generated in the ordinary course of business. Examples of those statutes include the Internal Revenue Code and Regulations, the Occupational and Hazards Act, the Age Discrimination and Employment Act of 1967, the Employee Retirement Income Security Act, the Immigration Reform and Control Act of 1986, the Family Medical Leave Act, and the Sarbanes-Oxley Act of 2002. Such retention requirements include electronic documents and e-mails. A very general rule for retention is nine years. However, it is wise to consult with your company's attorneys about any specific statutes specially affecting your company.

The duty to preserve documentation predates the filing of any formal litigation and arises when a party has notice or should have known the evidence might be relevant to future litigation. One of the best indicators is when there is some discussion that there might be a lawsuit or claim arising out of a particular incident. It is generally best to err on the side of caution. One of a litigator's greatest concerns is learning that a key employee has left, and that his or her computer has been allocated to someone else to use. That frequently results in overwriting of documents, which then are very costly to restore. If company personnel think a dispute is looming, care must be taken with respect to such computers.

Moreover, if the threat of a dispute is looming, a company must guard against the routine alteration or destruction of relevant documents. Instead, it must suspend document retention and destruction policy activities. The best method is to institute a "litigation hold" on all accessible data. Enforcement of that litigation hold is extremely important to avoid risk of a spoliation claim.

It is wise to use an outside computer consultant to help formulate a coherent strategy for the production of documents. Such a consultant should be knowledgeable and experienced in litigation matters. A specific person within the information technology staff should be designated to ensure that the policy is followed, and with management support. This will be frustrating to the company employees in the short run, but it will be gratifying if one knows what the alternative—spoliation instructions to the jury—could do to the company's future and prospects for successful resolution of the dispute.

The key to the strategy is ensuring that all the relevant documents have been gathered and stored in one place so the risk of loss or destruction is minimized. As noted above, this frequently will be resisted, or at least treated as a stepchild task, by company personnel because it takes them away from their other productive endeavors for their employer. A challenging part of the process is finding all the people with access to relevant data. It often is a mistake to rely on one person within the company to gather all the documents without involvement with litigation counsel asking questions of or about each person in the company. For example, several years ago a fellow lawyer with another firm told me about a situation in which, five months after his client (a large oil company) had assured him they had looked throughout the company for documents, he (the lawyer) happened while visiting the client offices to stumble across a special computer support office that had never been queried; having assured the opposing party and the judge five months earlier that all documents had been produced, to his great embarrassment and to the injury of the credibility of his client, he then had to produce a large volume of documents no one else had known about. So, having a strategy to perform a thorough search and analysis early in the case is very important.

Preserving Invention Rights

The advent of the Internet makes it surprisingly easy for engineers and financial personnel to unwittingly reveal valuable and competition-sensitive information to those outside the company. Companies that protect their competition-sensitive data are in a far better position to take advantage of the creativity and inventiveness of company personnel. It is wise business for companies to protect their trade secrets and patents.

A trade secret is any information that can be used in the operation of a business or other enterprise and that is sufficiently valuable and secret to afford an actual or potential advantage over others. A trade secret can consist of (a) a formula, (b) a pattern, (c) a compilation of data (including customer names and information), (d) a computer program, (e) a device or device design, (f) a method, technique, or process, or (g) other forms or embodiments of economically valuable information. Trade secrets can relate to technical matters such as composition or design of a product, a method of manufacturing, or the know-how necessary to perform a particular operation or service, pricing and marketing techniques, and the identity and special requirements of customers.

Often, trade secrets can relate to a new invention. Many inventions ultimately are protected by patents; however, while the new invention or process is being developed, as well as during the period while the patent application is pending, protection of the developments and design as trade secret and proprietary information is extremely important.

Steps to protect trade secrets include:

- Determine what really is a trade secret that really needs protecting.
- Stamp or label confidential/trade secret material or data as confidential.
- Enter into a confidentiality/non-disclosure agreement at the beginning of any discussion with anyone outside the company regarding your products/processes/information.

- Use passwords for your computers.
- Keep valuable data locked up.
- Enforce a "need to know" system when it comes to confidential information.
- Shred and securely dispose of hard copies of information that is being disposed of (don't just throw it in the trash can).
- Conduct proper background checks on new employees.
- Require all new employees to sign non-competition, non-disclosure, and/or trade secret confidentiality agreements when they start work.
- Require employees to update/sign new trade secret confidentiality/non-disclosure agreements annually.
- Conduct periodic, systematic audits and inventories of confidential information.
- Conduct exit interviews of every departing employee to ensure that all confidential information remains with the company.
- Bring lawsuits where necessary to protect trade secrets.

Patents

Patents benefit both the inventor and the public. Once issued, and subject to the payment of government fees, a patent gives an inventor the right to exclude others from making, using, or selling the patented invention for twenty years from the filing date of the application of the patent. A patent does not necessarily grant an absolute right to make or sell an invention; other impediments, such as someone else's patent that covers a key component of the invention, may stand in the way. The patent gives the public a set of illustrated instructions that explain how the invention works.

To be patentable, an invention must fall within at least one of the following categories:

- An article of manufacture
- A machine
- A process or method
- A composition of matter (a chemical compound)

- An improvement of any of the above
- An ornamental (non-functional) design of an article of manufacture
- An asexually reproduced plant

In addition, patentable inventions must be (a) new, (b) useful, and (c) non-obvious. Abstract ideas and scientific principles cannot be patented. They must first be embodied in a device or process that falls into one of the above classes.

Who May Patent?

Generally, only the inventor(s) may obtain a patent. (Of course, the inventor may assign the patent to someone else, such as an employer, who may seek the patent.) The invention must be the original idea of the inventor(s). The inventor may not have obtained the idea from others, and they must believe they are the first to independently conceive of the structure.

If an invention is successful, there can be protracted battles about who invented the item in question. It is therefore critical that inventors (and their companies) exercise care in sharing the work of the project and consider carefully the ramifications of discussing the work on the invention with others.

Who has the rights to the patent if the inventor works for a corporation, and does the corporation have any rights in the patent? The answer depends on whether the employee was initially hired or later directed to solve a specific problem or to exercise his or her inventive skills in a specific area. If the employee was hired, or later directed, to solve a specific problem to work on inventions in a specific area, the employer probably will have the right to claim the employee's inventions in that area as the company's. But if the employee was simply hired or directed to make improvements in a particular area, and if the corporation has not provided for the assignment of all inventions in an agreement with the employee, the corporation has no rights in the patent. However, even then the employer may have a "shop right" to use the invention if the employee used the employer's facilities to conceive or make the invention. The line between the two scenarios is not always clear, so it is wise to have an agreement with the employee specifically addressing the matter.

Losing Patent Rights

How can an inventor lose patent rights? In addition to abandonment by sale or offer of sale more than one year before the patent application, there are a number of ways in which an inventor can lose the opportunity to patent an invention, including but not limited to:

1. Failing to mark the product as covered by the patent
2. Failing to specify the "best mode" or embodiment of using the invention
3. Failing to provide a complete description of the invention in the patent application
4. Failing to reduce the invention to practice—that is, to a usable form
5. Failing to fairly and completely report the prior art so the Patent Office can determine if the invention really is new and non-obvious
6. Failing to patent the invention internationally (As a result, the invention may only be protected in this country.)

Copyright Manuals

Finally, it is wise to consider copyrighting the procedure, method, and equipment manuals. In certain circumstances, companies may want to copyright the manuals that are used in the public, distributed to customers, or even used internally to further preclude an employee from taking them and wholesale copying them for use at another company or in starting a new, competing business. For example, a manufacturer of compressors might want to copyright its equipment manuals so its competitors might be legally barred from wholesale copying of the manuals. In that manner, the competitor will have to expend its own funds developing or improving its own manuals instead of simply copying its competitor's. Whether a company's manuals can be protected through copyrights requires extensive discussion concerning authorship, "work for hire," and other issues.

For example, suppose your company initiates a new process for storing and transporting gas. You would not want an employee to leave and begin working for a competitor while bringing the manuals, created by your company at substantial expense and trouble, to simply be copied by the competitor. By providing copyright notice, and particularly if you register the copyright with the U.S. Copyright Office, if he or she and the new employer decide to save time and money by simply copying your manuals, thereby putting them at a competitive advantage because they do not have to create new manuals, you may sue to enjoin the use and for damages.

Clearly, copyrighting is an important part of the invention and overall business environment. Companies that rely on the goodwill of competitors and their current and former employees may be disappointed in the long run. Especially in this age of easy and quick e-mail communication, copyrighting is a critical tool in protecting an individual's or company's intellectual property.

Charles Frost graduated from the U.S. Military Academy at West Point (B.S. in general engineering, 1972), Savannah and Armstrong State Colleges (M.B.A., 1979), and the University of Texas School of Law (J.D., 1981). He also is a graduate of the U.S. Army Command and General Staff College, which is a multi-year course designed to teach the art and management of war.

After graduation from West Point, he served seven years in the U.S. Army as a combat arms officer (including service with the 1st Ranger Battalion and two company commands). After serving an additional nineteen and a half years in the Army Reserves, he retired with the rank of lieutenant colonel.

While in law school, Mr. Frost was a note editor on the Texas Law Review, *a successful moot court contestant and member of the Board of Advocates, and recipient of the award for the student who contributed the most to legal scholarship at the University of Texas Law School in 1981–1982. After completing his law studies at the University of Texas, he practiced primarily commercial and oil and gas litigation at one of the major Dallas law firms. In January of 1985, he returned to Houston (his hometown) and joined Chamberlain, Hrdlicka. He became a shareholder in January of 1989.*

Protecting an Energy Company's Intellectual Property

Mr. Frost's primary areas of practice are litigation of intellectual property, trade secrets, contracts, securities and business fraud, oil and gas, fiduciary duty, DTPA, anti-trust, patents, trademarks, copyrights, franchise, accountant liability/defense, and probate matters. His trial experience includes fraud, contract, securities, trade secrets, oil and gas, fiduciary duty, patent, libel and slander, probate, and covenant-not-to-compete litigation. He also has a developing sub-practice in intellectual property applications and confidentiality agreements.

Mr. Frost is a member of the commercial arbitrators ("neutrals") panel of the American Arbitration Association and successfully passed the examination to become an associate member of the Charter Institute of Arbitrators, headquartered in London, England. He is also a registered patent agent with the U.S. Patent Office.

On three occasions in the mid-1990s, Mr. Frost was appointed a master in County Court Number Four to handle the motions docket and discovery disputes. He has presented speeches at local Houston accountant seminars concerning contracts and fraud, intellectual property (trade secrets, patents, copyrights, and trademarks), the litigation process, and expert witnesses.

Mr. Frost was a director of the Houston Bar Association's litigation section in 2000–2002, a member of the State Bar College of Texas in 2001–03, and is listed in Marquis' Who's Who in American Law.

Dedication: *Joe H. Reynolds, Sidney B. Williams, and Paul E. Martin, who have mentored me over the past fifteen to twenty years and have taught me well, and my wife Judi, who encourages me each day to "go get some of those worms, and help people."*

Performing an Effective Cost/Benefit Analysis

Edward G. Kehoe
Partner
King & Spalding LLP

Commercial Energy Disputes Overview

As a commercial litigator, I represent clients in the energy industry who find themselves in business disputes, either as plaintiff or defendant in court, or as a claimant or respondent in arbitration. Energy disputes often arise from contracts that form the basis of an energy-related project. These agreements might include power purchase agreements, gas supply agreements, concession agreements, operation and maintenance agreements, and insurance policies (including performance standards and political risk). One or more parties to the dispute may be a governmental entity (which may implicate different laws), or the parties may be from the private sector. In this context, an energy dispute is similar to other commercial disputes that arise from contractual agreements. Nevertheless, energy disputes involve issues, terminology, and customs that are often unique to the energy industry, and a lawyer representing a client in a commercial energy dispute must be experienced with this industry if he or she is to be effective.

The terms of the contract from which the energy dispute arises normally will dictate the governing law and forum. Arbitration sometimes is particularly attractive to contracting parties who come from different countries.

Most commercial disputes, including those concerning energy matters, are settled prior to the trial or ultimate arbitration hearing on the merits. It is said that less than 5 percent of all commercial disputes proceed to an ultimate trial or arbitration hearing. Energy clients are in business to make money, not to devote time and money unnecessarily through protracted legal proceedings. I find that favorable settlements come from a position of strength. In this regard, it is important that the lawyer handling the case have substantial and real experience conducting an actual trial or arbitration proceeding. Many seasoned and senior litigators are quite talented at pre-trial matters such as strategy, brief writing, and discovery tactics. But because so many cases settle, these same lawyers have little or no actual experience conducting a trial or arbitration, which includes direct and cross-examination of witnesses. As the scheduled date for trial or hearing approaches, a client whose lawyer is not perfectly comfortable in a trial or arbitration hearing setting normally will be somewhat less aggressive during settlement discussions. Of course, if the case does not settle, the client who is represented by counsel who has substantial trial and arbitration hearing experience will have an advantage over one that does not. Sophisticated energy companies know this, and they select legal counsel accordingly.

Clarity of Contract

There is one significant energy-related issue that transcends the rest, and this is the clarity of the contract. Disputes sometimes arise when events transpire within the contractual relations that were not contemplated by the parties at the time they drafted their agreement. Similarly, disputes arise when the terms of the contract are ambiguous, and the ambiguity has a financial impact on the ultimate performance of the contract. If a contract becomes less profitable (or unprofitable) for a party, contract language that appeared clear earlier comes under scrutiny. If the language is not perfectly clear on the relevant issue, a dispute likely will arise. The key, of course, is clarity at the outset. Clarity of contract includes recognition by the contract drafters that the person or persons who ultimately will decide a dispute likely will not be an expert on energy industry issues. Terms that are familiar to industry participants will be foreign to decision-makers when a dispute goes to trial or arbitration hearing, and different interpretations of the term may be advanced at trial or arbitration. Where possible, drafters of contracts should be sensitive to this fact and choose language with requisite specificity to avoid alternative interpretations.

Cost/Benefit Analysis

Litigation and arbitration of energy disputes involves risk. There is no guarantee of outcome. Clients are not experts at assessing this risk—that is what they pay me to do for them, and it is an important task that I perform as early in the case as possible. I work hard at the outset of a case to gain a good understanding of the documents, facts, and law from the perspective of my client and my adversary. From this I try to provide my client with a reasonable assessment of the likely outcome of the case. Of course, this is not an exact science, and certain facts may not be known until a later stage of the case. In that eventuality, I may not be able to provide an early assessment, or my initial assessment may change. But normally I can get a very good sense of a case early on. I often provide this preliminary assessment in terms of a percentage. For example, one of my clients recently was accused of breaching a power purchase agreement, and the plaintiff claimed many millions of dollars in damages. I advised the client that based on my preliminary review of the facts and law, the client had a 70 percent probability of success in an ultimate trial of the matter. By success I meant the client would pay no damages because it did not breach the contract as alleged by the plaintiff. I also provided a rough estimate of the legal fees and costs (as well as the fees of expert witnesses) to bring the case through a trial.

With this information, the client was able to perform a cost/benefit analysis of litigating the dispute versus attempting to settle the dispute early in the process. It also provided the client with a good framework within which to determine its settlement offer. The client understood and considered that it had a 30 percent chance of paying a substantial money judgment (and that legal and expert fees would be incurred along the way), and the client made a fair settlement offer that included all estimated legal and expert costs plus a premium associated with the 30 percent risk of loss. The plaintiff rejected the offer. We proceeded through document exchange, depositions, and other discovery, and no additional material facts were revealed. The client repeated its settlement offer, and it was again rejected. We tried the case to a jury and won. The total cost to the client was legal and expert fees—not the previously offered premium. That is the way a cost/benefit analysis should work. The client made the right cost/benefit decision at each step in the process and reaped the financial reward of prudent business decisions, based on early legal advice that looked well forward.

Knowledge

In order to advise the client with a litigation/arbitration cost/benefit analysis, and to effectively represent the client if the case does not settle, I stay abreast of trends in the energy industry. I do this mainly by staying close to my clients and advising them periodically on various issues that arise. I find that this helps keep me abreast of the industry. Having active cases helps one to stay current. In addition to staying active in work itself, I also keep current on industry issues through membership in industry legal groups, attending seminars, and reading industry publications. My firm has an e-mail publication system that includes a group of people who do related work, and who receive recent case rulings and developments by periodic e-mail messages. This helps keep us informed of new developments and decisions.

Settlement Negotiations

In my profession as a commercial litigator/arbitrator, negotiations take place in a dispute setting. I do not negotiate contracts the way a transactional lawyer does, but I do negotiate on behalf of my clients throughout the litigation or arbitration process. In litigation and arbitration, there are negotiations over many things, such as which documents you agree to produce to the other side, the number of depositions (and the individuals from the client organization who will be subject to deposition), and potential settlement of the case. My strategy for negotiating settlement of the case is to know the law and the facts, because knowledge is power. It is essential to present your position during settlement talks clearly, precisely, and effectively, and then counter the opponent's points clearly and concisely. This is particularly important if my opponent's client is participating in the settlement discussions, such as during a mediation. This may be the first time the opponent's client is made aware of the facts and issues favoring our side.

At the same time, however, it is never possible to win every point. I like to go into a negotiation and disarm the opposing side by conceding points. Throughout the negotiation and discussion process, I slowly acknowledge and concede, while I simultaneously stress the important points that tilt the balance in my favor. I think there is a good credibility and sense of power in this.

The hardest point on which to find a middle ground with the other side in settlement, and sometimes even your own client, is almost always money. Most people do not care, in principle, which party is right or wrong; they just want their money. I find that in negotiations it is usually not too difficult to get the other side to appreciate their weaknesses, and we can appreciate our own. The difficulty lies in getting from the last offer made to the settlement the client is really looking for. I believe this is a function of creating a heightened perception of risk in the mind of the other party. The art of the negotiations at this point in the process is convincing the other lawyer (and client) that my client and I are fully prepared to go to trial or arbitration hearing. This is not a bluff. The other side will sense this conviction, because it is real. From there, I further try to impress on the opponent that if the case does proceed to trial or arbitration hearing, we will win and he or she will lose. This approach sounds basic and simple, because it is.

Advice to Clients

One piece of important advice I give clients is that its commitment and close involvement in the litigation or arbitration will increase the likelihood of success. In the end, a trial or arbitration comes down to witness testimony. Effective witnesses win cases, and ineffective witnesses lose cases. A corporation must make its employees and potential witnesses available to work with the lawyers at length to prepare the case. The employees have insights into the business that the lawyer lacks, and the employees will educate the lawyer as to the facts. The lawyer, on the other hand, will teach and bond with the witness. The more time they spend together, the better the witness is likely to perform at trial. I have seen time and time again that clients who actively participate in the litigation reap the reward in a favorable verdict. A client who is unable or unwilling to dedicate significant time to a litigation or arbitration matter should factor that into settlement decisions.

Edward Kehoe is a partner in the New York litigation group of King & Spalding LLP. He has significant experience representing clients in a wide variety of business litigation matters, specializing in disputes between parties in the energy and oil and gas industries. Mr. Kehoe regularly represents clients in federal and state court actions, in arbitrations, and before governmental bodies. Clients also rely upon Mr. Kehoe to provide strategic advice for effective and efficient resolution at early stages of a dispute, and to conduct internal investigations when necessary.

Mr. Kehoe has been a frequent lecturer on business litigation issues. He has spoken at the Third Annual Power Industry Forum in Amelia Island, Florida; the King & Spalding Executive Briefing Luncheon at the Waldorf Astoria in New York City; the Eleventh Annual Fall Conference of the Independent Power Producers of New York in Albany, New York; and the Seventeenth Annual National Conference of Bankruptcy Judges in San Diego, California.

Performing an Effective Cost/Benefit Analysis

Mr. Kehoe, a native of Mahopac, New York, received a bachelor's degree in accounting from Lehigh University in 1987. At Lehigh, he was an NCAA all-American track runner, and he received the university's award as the outstanding scholar and athlete. Mr. Kehoe received his J.D., cum laude, from St. John's Law School in 1990 and was a member of the St. John's Law Review. Before joining King & Spalding in 1993, Mr. Kehoe was with the firm of Skadden, Arps, Slate, Meagher & Flom in New York. He is admitted to practice in the federal and New York state courts, and before the U.S. Court of Appeals, District of Columbia Circuit.

Getting to Know the Client

Frank A. Caro Jr.
Shareholder
Polsinelli Shalton Welte Suelthaus PC

Energy Law: An Overview

Energy law is among the most dynamic areas of legal practice today, as scientific discoveries and environmental concerns constantly change the legal environment for energy providers and their customers. As an energy law attorney whose clients are largely public utilities, I specialize in up-to-date, accurate knowledge and insightful strategies concerning state regulatory practice as well as mergers and acquisitions. I assist my clients in planning for the future, ensuring that they meet current regulatory standards, and merging and acquiring assets without encountering legal problems.

Dealing with regulatory laws is a complex process with far-reaching effects. Each state possesses its own regulatory provisions, as does the federal government. Often, energy industry clients confront issues in both federal and state regulatory forums, as many transactions affect various states and involve issues effecting interstate commerce where federal jurisdiction issues are concerned. Over the past fifteen years, many of these regulatory provisions have been transformed as politicians, industry leaders, and public interest groups attempt to change the economic regulation of energy providers. Unprepared utilities can find these transformations highly disruptive; energy law attorneys, therefore, try to anticipate changes and devise plans that ease their clients into efficient operation under new regulations.

For instance, the law typically mandates that a utility wishing to adjust its rates must file a rate case, evaluating its situation and arguing the need for the adjustment. Rate cases, however, are expensive and time-consuming. Utilities can avoid such cases under certain adjustment provisions, such as weather normalization adjustments, which allow utilities to adjust their rates in order to recover costs caused by adverse weather. An attorney who knows how such provisions apply can help his or her client devise a regulatory plan that allows it to adjust rates based on a weather formula without having to file a rate case.

Similarly, a utility that is building a $1.3 billion power plant can, working with its attorney, develop a resource and regulatory plan to build or acquire those assets without suffering a major financial impact to its bond ratings.

By showing the need for more power in an area and ensuring that it has the cash flow to meet its financial requirements, the utility can work within regulations to provide power to customers without impairing its financial condition. The development of such a plan requires:

- Full understanding of your client's risks and goals
- Understanding various parties' issues and concerns
- Knowledge of regulatory laws and various hot topics

At times, the most effective regulatory strategy is to attempt to change the regulations themselves. For instance, if the price of natural gas rises, a utility may need to drill more wells in an area where the state restricts the production of natural gas. The utility's lawyer could then research the restrictions and, through discussion with the regulators or the legislature, attempt to alter the regulations to reflect the changed environment caused by the rising gas prices. The positive effects of such proactive measures are long-term and widespread, but their success depends upon the attorney's ability to convince the relevant political entities that the utility's goals are beneficial to the community. Legislative changes require a concise explanation that:

1. Changed economic conditions exist and old laws are no longer useful.
2. Changes are beneficial to the state's policies and citizens.
3. Changes would create a partnership between business and government, creating a win-win situation.

Mergers and acquisitions are increasingly prevalent in the energy business: more and more energy companies are merging and acquiring assets, as well as becoming involved in telecommunications and power trading. However, due in part to harmful alliances such as those involved in the Enron case, there is also a trend toward diversification, which in turn has resulted in political changes that allow utilities to merge or acquire each other in different manners. We attempt to take these issues into account when structuring a transaction and ensure that both companies are getting the best possible outcome from the deal. Understanding each original company allows us to address potential problems before the merger, and better handle the final, blended entity.

Knowledge of regulatory issues is also an asset when handling mergers and acquisitions. Due to political restrictions on alliances between energy providers, completing a transaction may require a company to file for a rate increase, decrease its rates, or otherwise make adjustments that may affect the economics of the deal. Non-regulatory legal issues also play a part, as they do in all mergers and acquisitions: matters of due diligence, indemnity, and contractual obligations are equally important in the energy business.

Whether a utility is seeking financing to develop alternative sources of power, trying to recover costs caused by weather, or attempting to avoid regulatory lag on a major construction project, its broad goal is always the same: to provide customers with more efficient service and to increase its profits in order to grow as a company. By understanding this goal, as well as a client's more tactical objectives, and the environment in which the client must seek them, an energy law attorney may bring experience and knowledge to bear on a case. Working as a strategic partner with a client, developing a plan and investigating the means to carry it out, is my optimal and most effective role.

Working with Clients

Part of a partnership with a client is knowledge of its ultimate goal. When I'm aware of a client's aspirations for five or ten years in the future, I'm better equipped to see how the current situation can change to serve this long-term plan. Furthermore, I can then assist the client in strategizing for its future goals: setting benchmarks, evaluating the environment, and investigating impediments and the means by which they can be overcome.

Utilities' goals frequently include major transactions: mergers and acquisitions, strategic alliances, building and development plans, and attempted regulatory changes. Such transactions can require the approval of a utility's board of directors, its shareholders, its customers, regulatory bodies, and the public. It's thus vital for a utility to first determine the advantage it's seeking from a transaction, then discover ways the transaction can benefit other bodies as well. At times, it may be necessary to make slight alterations in the interest of the public or of regulatory bodies, such as pledging some of the transaction's profit to community service.

The regulatory process involves both patience and persistence. However, it's also flexible, and a utility that works at its pace without giving up is likely to achieve its goals in the end, provided that those goals are clear, defined, and realistic. New companies, that don't understand the patience required or the need for multiple approvals, are more likely to create problems for themselves via impatience or oversight than those that are willing to see the process through without rushing.

Clarity is also necessary when dealing with energy law. Each transaction has many constituencies, such as the board of directors and the regulatory agency, and each has its own goals and concerns. Understanding them allows an attorney to create a solid and compelling case. This knowledge should begin with, and be most extensive about, the client: if a client can articulate its plans, an attorney, working within them, can structure a plan that meets everyone's needs.

Advice

Effective energy law practice depends on knowing the changes in the field. For example, the Energy Policy Act of 2005 has been a recent topic of discussion; it's a provision that will shape a great deal of future energy law, and it's important to understand both its various aspects and its evolution and changes over the last five or six years. Lawyers who are familiar with the act will be able to advise their clients on how best to work within it and ensure compliance before problems arise. As new political and environmental concerns affect the energy business, a successful energy attorney is one who is on the edge of current changes and aware of the probable future.

Keeping up with these changes requires a lawyer to be proactive and involved with his or her community. I participate in trade groups such as the Midwest Energy Association, the Energy Bar Association, and the American Gas Association; I also subscribe to a number of publications that keep me abreast of trends in both clients and the industry. Finally, I talk frequently with clients, discussing their goals, changes in the industry, and how to integrate the two for maximum efficiency.

The best piece of advice I've received in my practice is to be the lawyer who finds a way to complete a client's goal, not the one to tell the client its goals are impossible. The industry is heavily regulated, but the flexibility of those regulations means a creative, innovative lawyer can find a way to accomplish almost anything. When a client has a goal, its attorney should be willing to create a solution to see that goal fulfilled.

For clients, my advice is to have patience at all times. Their frustration is often understandable, as the industry frequently puts complicated regulations in the path of their goals. However, patience and persistence, when working with various groups, can lead to a settlement worth much more than litigation.

Political concerns for the environment, the consumers, and competition aren't going to disappear, and neither will the regulation they cause. In order to deal with that regulation while still maintaining efficiency and profits, utilities and their attorneys must work in close partnerships, finding ways to obey the laws and still meet their goals.

Viewing a New Case

Planning for the future depends highly on understanding the past, especially in a highly regulated industry such as energy. Past issues can create problems in new transactions or expose clients to litigation and even criminal charges. Therefore, my first priority, when meeting a new client, is to assess its potential exposure to legal issues.

The first step in the process is understanding the client's goals, some of which the client may not think to mention. Some clients don't see their situations from a larger perspective or don't think that perspective is important; the attorney, however, must always attempt to assemble the pieces and view the big picture. A client may not understand the financial implications of a transaction or the alternatives to the way it's handling the matter. In these cases, an attorney must ask questions, bring up alternative methods, and search for weaknesses.

Weaknesses can include problematic relationships with customers, politicians, shareholders, or even partners; a variety of individuals who have their reasons to be unhappy about the manner in which the utility does business. Dealing with them may entail structuring a transaction differently or compromising with a difficult party on another matter to make sure the utility can reach its goal. All need to be dealt with, however, and doing so requires understanding. I, therefore, always ask a new client about the circumstances of a transaction: what businesses or communities the plan will affect, why the client believes it to be a good idea, and which individuals might think otherwise.

When taking on a new client or case, knowledge is key. Being aware of issues allows an attorney to address them proactively and perhaps gain closure on them in a manner that will disrupt neither a client's current business nor its future goals. It's therefore vital that an attorney discover all possible information about a client and a case before moving forward.

Recent Changes

The energy business doesn't have its roots in competition: until the 1980s, the government regulated utilities, maintaining stability and preventing competition. Deregulation in the 1980s allowed many new parties to enter the marketplace; it also, however, created the potential for catastrophic failures, which went largely unrecognized until the Enron crisis. Since Enron, many energy companies have failed or become financially weaker, and the field is only now starting to recover.

Evolution and change continues in the energy business. Competition has led to increased diversification, as companies attempt to gain the edge on one another by filling different niches. With the memory of Enron, however, they're more cautious and aware of the risks: in the twenty-first century, competition is more measured and structured than was the case in the late 1990s. Going forward, I believe technology will continue to drive change and create opportunities and efficiencies in the energy industry. I also believe the heightened awareness of our environment will also move us forward.

The Three Golden Rules of Energy Law

Understand the regulatory challenges in the energy industry–by keeping abreast of changes in the industry. Understand your clients' goals and objectives, and help them focus and articulate those objectives in clear and concise statements. Help your clients understand that patience and persistence are the keys to successful regulatory outcomes.

Concentrating his practice in the energy/utility and telecommunications industries, Frank Caro offers his clients vast experience in business regulatory and governmental affairs. His experience in the electric, gas, and telecommunications industries has assisted clients in structuring complex regulatory solutions to difficult problems.

Prior to joining the firm, Mr. Caro served as general counsel for the Kansas Corporation Commission and acted as chief trial counsel in numerous hearings before that commission, the Federal Energy Regulatory Commission, and the Federal Communications Commission. He represents clients involved in all phases of energy/utility and telecommunications industries from producers to consumers, from investor-owned utilities to electric cooperatives.

Mr. Caro represents clients before the Missouri Public Service Commission and the Kansas Corporation Commission on various matters involving certification proceedings, mergers and acquisitions, rate tariff applications, generic rule-making proceedings, and complaints. He serves as general regulatory counsel for numerous public utilities.

During the past ten years, he was successful in assisting a client in the drafting and numerous enactments of legislation in Kansas that reforms the entire regulatory scheme of the telecommunications and CATV industry.

Recently, Mr. Caro assisted a client in completing the first phase of a $1.3 billion infrastructure development and regulatory plan for a major electric utility in the region that encompasses a new base load coal plant, significant environmental upgrades, and wind power.

Bringing the Deal to Closure: The Ultimate Goal

Todd Culwell
Partner
Pillsbury Winthrop Shaw Pittman LLP

As an energy lawyer, I work in three main areas: energy infrastructure project development and finance, energy infrastructure project acquisitions and divestitures, and general energy finance. The energy infrastructure projects include all aspects of upstream oil and gas projects, midstream projects, and downstream projects. Upstream projects range from the development of oil and gas platforms to just the financing of producing oil and gas properties. Midstream projects include pipelines, gas separation facilities, and gas liquefaction facilities, while downstream projects include chemical plants in which natural gas is the primary throughput (such as methanol or ammonia), power plants, or liquefied natural gas receiving terminals.

Energy infrastructure project development includes all aspects of developing a project, which begins with land acquisition, engineering, procurement and construction contracts, throughput supply agreements, and operation and maintenance agreements, and ends with the sale of the ultimate product of the facility.

I believe our greatest strength is in energy infrastructure development, and this is where we add the most value for our clients. In the energy infrastructure development area, it is important to have someone who is familiar with all aspects of these agreements and is able to synthesize and allocate risk in each of these contracts, especially from a commercial perspective. When a large energy infrastructure project is being developed, the commercial specialist may be divided up based upon the various commercial specialties. Similarly, this can happen on the legal side where lawyers with specialties in a legal discipline handle specific contractual arrangements. I believe it is very important to have at least one lawyer who is familiar with every contractual relationship of a transaction and can make each contract work together, or understand where there are gaps and explain those gaps to the commercial team to make an informed commercial decision on risk allocation. There will always be subtle risk allocation issues that must be dealt with in all contracts, and if they are handled incorrectly, there can be serious consequences. Thus, it is important to ensure that everyone understands how risks are allocated, to maintain consistency in the way they are allocated and to come to a commercial consensus for the final allocation.

Bringing the Deal to Closure: The Ultimate Goal

My practice also includes representation of clients in connection with the acquisition or divestiture of energy infrastructure projects.

The final piece of my practice relates to financing, either representing the lenders or a borrower. My finance practice relates to limited recourse project financing, where the owners or sponsors of a project invest in a project company. In these cases, lenders typically cannot look beyond the project company revenues for repayment of the debt. I also deal with basic energy finance for producing properties or services companies. Unlike project finance, where all decisions are based upon the revenues of a particular project, basic energy financing involves financing based on a company's balance sheet or particular assets mortgaged to the lenders.

Equity Financing Versus Project Financing

The potential financial implications of energy law will depend upon the size of the client. A large, international oil and gas company will view its deals differently than independent, mid-size, or smaller companies. The size of the company often changes the manner in which projects are analyzed and financed—whether it be equity financing, whereby a company pays with equity off of its own balance sheet, or debt financing, where banks take the risk. Of course, the risk profile will change based upon the type of lender. A major oil company will often pursue joint ventures with other companies that do not have as strong of a balance sheet.

Yet while some large companies will do project financing, other major companies do not have any interest in doing so because of the time and expense. This means a company may finance a project completely with equity, yet still maintain the mindset that it will, at some point, be converted to a project financing. Smaller companies like Chenier Energy, which is a small, public company, usually require arranging debt financing before commencement of construction. On the other hand, a major oil and gas company could complete 80 percent or more of its construction with only equity funding. Ultimately, once a project financing is completed, the major oil and gas company will be able to acquire, in the form of a dividend, its funded equity portion.

The strategy behind getting a project done is different based upon whether a company is using equity financing or debt financing. Being comfortable that a company can finance it with equity makes the process simpler, because it does not need a third-party lender advising as to the structure. But even in these cases, such a company must keep in mind that a third-party lender will step in at some point, so it is important to have the documents prepared in such a way that the project could be financed in the future with debt financing.

Risk Allocation

Many times, large, international companies pursuing the larger energy transactions are just as sophisticated as many of their outside counsel. Companies will not pursue anything if they do not have a solid understanding of the risk, or when risk has not been allocated as anticipated. This can mean a three-feet-tall stack of documents must be sorted through to make sure there is no risk being inadvertently taken or, in some cases, not taken. Even risks that are not taken as intended can ultimately impact the cost of the project.

The goal is not always to say, "I want to allocate liabilities away from my company," because often that is not the most efficient way to complete a project—for example, with respect to a construction contractor, the counterparty to the engineering, procurement, and construction (EPC) contract. A project sponsor will typically try to push as many of the risks as possible to the EPC contractor in order to make the contract financeable for a future lender. However, the ramification of such an allocation of risk is that the EPC contract is ultimately going to cost more for the EPC contractor to assume such risk. It is critical to keep in mind the friction that, by pushing risk away from the project company, will likely increase the ultimate capital cost of a project. The major oil and gas companies often prefer to retain the risk at the project company level and reduce the cost of the project.

The major issue is making sure all parties agree as to how they intended to allocate the risk. It is also possible to run into trouble when, somewhere in that three-feet-tall stack of documents, a negotiated change is made that reverberates throughout other agreements in unanticipated ways. This often happens as the project proceeds to transaction, when all parties are pushing to get the agreement signed. It is important to read through all documents thoroughly in order to ensure consistency in the agreed risk allocation.

The Key to a Successful Deal: Adequate Structuring

Success in my role is dictated by adequately documenting the agreed deal and by making sure my client is aware of how the legal interpretation could ultimately impact the agreed commercial transaction. In other words, you must reflect the deal in the documents by fleshing out the details with your client and making certain that everyone understands those details. The process often starts with the basic concepts outlined in a memorandum of understanding or letter of intent, which should be thoroughly analyzed as to how they impact the project. Adequately structuring the deal, and keeping an open dialogue with your client along the way, are vital.

I don't think being slick with your contracts is necessarily a success. In these cases, you have basically convinced the other side that you have something hidden in the documents, and that they will be taking a risk they did not anticipate taking. Making your documents so complicated that you are the only one who truly understands them, and using that to push things off to other parties, is no way to do a deal. If you have pushed a risk away from your client and to the other side in such a way that the other side did not agree to it in a knowledgeable manner, you will ultimately end up in a dispute when that risk comes to fruition.

Adequately structuring and papering a transaction in such a way that it reflects everyone's intent will limit disputes in the future. Many of these contracts are very complicated, and even with so many stacks and reams of paper, it is impossible to document every potential risk. If you can come to an agreement on how those risks will be addressed, and both sides can agree after the deal is done without going into any kind of dispute resolution process, I consider that a successful deal.

Maintaining Consistency: Keeping Yourself Involved

From a strategy standpoint, I try to be as hands-on as possible with my clients. I try not to pigeonhole myself into one piece of a deal, relying solely on someone else to complete the other pieces. It can be more efficient to bring your very best EPC person in on an engineering construction project, but if that person does not know how the output contract works or how all the contracts fit together, it will not matter even if he or she is the best EPC person in the world. Ultimately, he or she will not work as well as having someone who is involved in every aspect of the deal.

Thus, even when you bring in specialists, it is important to keep yourself involved in every aspect of the deal. This ensures that when an issue arises in one contract, you will be able to guide an agreement on how to address that issue in all the other agreements. Without having someone who is consistently and actively involved in every piece of the deal, you will run the risk of inconsistency.

Settlements and Negotiations

In negotiations, I try to be accommodating, yet not so accommodating as to be a detriment to my client. It is crucial to maintain open communications with each side and to avoid confrontation when there is no need for it. Negotiations are often simply a matter of agreeing on how a risk will be addressed and the best way to document and structure it. I don't find it to be helpful at all when the lawyers on both sides are confrontational, and I never try to impress my clients by making things difficult for the other side.

If I see issues I feel the other side does not understand how to address fairly, I will raise the issue so everyone is on the same page. If you operate this way from the beginning to the end of the negotiation process, I believe you will ultimately come out with a better product. To the extent that you can avoid confrontational attitudes, the contract negotiation process will be as enjoyable as possible. This means it is key to understand all the various pieces of a deal, how they fit together, and how to work with the other side to make sure it is all papered properly.

Key Parties

When you are working with a major oil company, you will often find that the manner in which the deal is structured and negotiated is such that you will work with very different people on very different pieces of the deal.

BRINGING THE DEAL TO CLOSURE: THE ULTIMATE GOAL

Each person brings expertise on various areas in the deal, and they will step in and out as needed. Major companies will handle most of their work in-house. With smaller or independent companies, you will usually deal with one commercial person from beginning to end, with perhaps one or two in-house counsel.

Who you deal with will also depend upon the type of project you are working on. I work with my former firm on quite a few deals, and I try to refer deals to them because I know we have similar negotiation styles. Whenever you have that, it can make for a better final project and a more efficient outside counsel on both ends. Thus, it limits the fees on a deal and makes for a quicker closing if you have the right lawyers on the other side as well.

Commonly Negotiated Items

In an acquisition or disposition agreement, the indemnities are always negotiated heavily, yet in actuality it becomes a commercial issue on how the indemnities work. Some of the biggest negotiation issues in these agreements have to do with certainty of closing. If you are selling an infrastructure project, you want to be sure you will ultimately reach a closure on the deal, so often your closing conditions will be a significant negotiating point.

Of course, calling closing conditions a big negotiating point also implicates every other piece of the agreement, since it impacts how you negotiate your represents and warranties in order for them to be true to close. Thus, as a seller, you must be very careful that you have structured the agreement in such a way that you get as close to certainty to closure as you possibly can. This means the indemnities and deductibles are heavily negotiated, particularly in terms of the links that can be brought once an indemnity claim has been made. Many times, the indemnities are structured so that a claim cannot be brought until it has surpassed a certain amount—in other words, there is a deductible. These are very commercial in nature, and so it is an issue that arises even in warranty negotiation settings.

The first step is to negotiate closing conditions, making sure you will reach closure, and the conditions under which you have the right to terminate or walk away from a deal. Again, these issues reverberate throughout your represents and warranties. You must be careful in granting the other side the opportunity to walk away, because once you have locked up your project and signed the agreement, you cannot continue to sell it. If you spend six months trying to get a closure and ultimately do not reach it because you have given the other side the right to walk away from the deal, the transaction will fail. Therefore, being able to take a project to closure at least on an acquisition or divestiture deal is a critical issue and hotly negotiated.

From a project financing standpoint, a similar issue arises surrounding when you can draw down money under your financing agreement. This is similar to closing conditions in that you must outline certain conditions that must be satisfied in order to make a drawing, and they are likewise the subject of much negotiation. Of course, you want to be sure you have the ability to access your debt when and as needed, but the effects of what is negotiated also echoes throughout other areas of the agreement. This particularly relates to covenants in terms of where you are in connection with your project, and whether you have been in compliance with all your covenants. If, as the borrower's council, you are unable to make a drawing because there is an unanticipated issue that keeps the drawing from taking place, your negotiations cannot be said to have been successful.

Distinct Issues in Energy Law Negotiations

Energy law is somewhat unique in that it requires a strong understanding of the energy industry itself. Let's say you are buying or selling a company that sells medical products. The more you know about medical products, the better your position will be in negotiating the deal, but this is not to say you must be an expert in the medical products field to do a reasonably good job.

Likewise, it is not necessary to be an expert in every aspect of an energy transaction, but you must be able to understand the basic industry. It may not be necessary to worry about gas marketing issues in terms of how gas is sold in the United States, for example, but the echoes of those issues will be seen throughout the contract. If you are not generally familiar with the gas marketing mechanics during a gas or an L&G deal, you will run yourself into trouble. A contract whose ultimate goal is to build an L&G receiving terminal in the United States, whereby the product will be put into a U.S. pipeline system, necessitates an understanding of how gas marketing has worked in this country for the past ten to fifteen years. Going back to our previous example of the medical device company representative, I believe it would be harder for that person to step into energy law than it would be for an energy lawyer to step into a medical device deal.

Research and Preparation

One must be extremely prepared in terms of the document itself that is being negotiated, as well as the other agreements that relate to that document. Thus, you must understand the other agreements that work together with the document. It is often helpful to talk with the other partners in the specific areas you are negotiating in order to get a good understanding of what is considered market.

Identifying the market standard is key to certain negotiation points. For example, if you have a deductible for your indemnity in a purchase and sale agreement, you want to have an idea of the market in terms of what people will accept. Usually, this is a percentage of your purchase price. Figuring out the right percentage is one area in which you can add value to the business side, if you yourself have done many transactions and if you have access to people in your law firm who also have that experience. Of course, there will be times when you have many more transactions under your belt than your client does, and there will be times when the opposite is true. Regardless, being able to bring an understanding of what the current market is on various negotiated issues before you walk in the door is very helpful.

The points that are hardest to bridge will always be the last ones that are negotiated. I have found that it truly varies depending upon what kind of transaction it is, and each deal will have hot buttons. If you are working on a project that has significant environmental issues, which can be particularly difficult to agree upon, it may keep you from signing the deal. Many times, it will be impossible to reach a consensus on how to allocate those risks, and one must be prepared for this outcome.

Settlement Issues: The Importance of Dispute Resolution Specialists

I myself do not do litigation, but I have been involved in projects for which we try to reach a settlement on issues that pop up during the construction phase, before the project is complete. This situation arises when projects move forward into construction despite the fact that issues have not been addressed as people wanted them to be. Ultimately, it is necessary to sit down with the contractor and walk through a settlement procedure to put an end to the issue in contention. These are short-term contracts in that they take two to three years to construct and have a one- to two-year warranty period.

Naturally, these situations are much more adversarial. Usually, an adversarial or dispute resolution specialist is brought in, since it is much different than negotiating a contract. The process involves a commercial lawyer, like myself, sitting in with a dispute resolution specialist in order to hammer out the agreement. My role would simply be to help document the ultimate settlement.

Particularly in adversarial situations such as these, it is critical to bring in the right people who have proper experience in adversarial dealings on a daily basis. Lawyers like myself are used to working in a team setting to reach closure, rather than trying to better the other side. This is a major difference between transactional and dispute resolution law.

Measures of Success

One obvious indicator that you are successful at what you are doing is repeat business from your existing clients. Yet I believe that if someone from the other side of a deal is impressed by your handling of a deal and asks you to represent them on another deal, it is even more indicative of success. This has happened to me a few times, and I attribute it to the fact that I am not difficult to deal with. I am open and accessible, and I do not engage in games or tricks. People hire me to get their deals done, and my goal is always to bring a deal to closure.

I consider myself a deal lawyer, which requires a good deal of skill in problem resolution. Ultimately, what I bring to the deal is an ease of closure without a great deal of pain and suffering on any one side. Because I am easy to deal with from both sides, I would not say the other side of the table would consider me a painful lawyer to deal with, which can be a significant handicap to communication.

Todd Culwell joined the firm in October of 2005 as a partner in the Houston office. His practice includes the representation of developers in connection with domestic and international infrastructure project development and project financings, including drafting and negotiating of project development documentation (joint venture, engineering/procurement/construction, throughput, and off-take agreements), bank and capital market financing documentation, and coordination with local counsel. Mr. Culwell completed a two-year, in-house secondment with the Middle East group of an international energy company. His experience also includes representation of companies in connection with various forms of dispositions and acquisitions of energy infrastructure assets.

Mr. Culwell also focuses on the representation of financial institutions and borrowers in a variety of corporate financing activities, including general commercial lending (ranging from complex syndicated loans with multiple currencies and tranches to single-lender loans), acquisition financing, oil and gas financing, letter of credit facilities, leveraged leasing transactions covering a variety of plants and equipment, various structured financing transactions (including volumetric production payments, prepaid forward contracts, and receivables financing), financings in connection with industrial revenue bonds, and representation of corporate trusts with the issuance of collateralized bond obligations.

Mr. Culwell earned his J.D., magna cum laude, in 1993 from the South Texas College of Law and his B.A. in economics in 1990 from the University of Texas at Austin.

Energy Regulation and Policy in a Time of Change: A Modest Agenda for Utility Regulators, an Ambitious Agenda for Federal Policymakers

Jeffrey D. Komarow
Partner
Bradley Arant Rose & White LLP

A Summary of Energy Law

Energy law is the application of legal principles (contracts, torts, etc.) and skills (contract drafting, litigation, etc.) to provide a legal framework for the production, transportation, and delivery of various forms of energy—primarily fossil energy (oil, natural gas, and coal), nuclear, hydro, and other forms of renewable energy and electricity.[1] To me, the most fascinating aspect of energy law is its diversity. An energy lawyer may find himself or herself negotiating the terms for the construction and financing of a new power plant or natural gas pipeline; representing a utility or its customers in a regulatory proceeding involving the rates, terms, and conditions of service at the federal or state level; representing a party in a commercial dispute over the sale of energy; or seeking to shape legislation or regulatory policy. The Energy Policy Act of 2005 (Pub Law 109-58) enacted on July 29, 2005, (EPACT 2005) reflects the length and breadth of energy law. The legislation contains eighteen titles that directly affect renewable energy (including geothermal, hydro, and hydrogen), oil and natural gas, coal, and nuclear. It contains tax and regulatory incentives to promote energy efficiency. EPACT 2005 also addresses industry structure in numerous important ways, including giving the Federal Energy Regulatory Commission (FERC) increased authority and clout to prevent market manipulation such as occurred in the California electricity market, repealing the Public Utility Holding Company Act of 1935, and giving the FERC authority to approve public utility mergers. Ultimately, however, EPACT 2005 legislates at the margin and fails to take bold action to counteract the nation's addiction to fossil energy, particularly oil, through increased efficiency, conservation, and increased exploration and development, particularly offshore on the Atlantic and Pacific coasts where any commercial discoveries could be quickly delivered to market.

As we enter the second half of the first decade of the twenty-first century, the country has already seen an energy crisis in California caused by myriad factors including manipulation of poorly thought out, pseudo-competitive

---

[1] Note that electricity is derivative. We convert the primary forms of energy into electricity in the process of generation. For example, with fossil fuels and nuclear, we convert thermal energy into electricity. With types of renewable energy, such as hydro and wind, the energy source is harnessed directly to turn generators and produce electricity.

market structure rules; the rise and spectacular fall of Enron Corporation, the nation's largest energy trading firm; the near collapse of the market for independent power generation with numerous bankruptcies, including bankruptcy filings by Mirant Corporation, Calpine Corporation, and others; a major blackout in the Midwest and Northeast; unprecedented energy infrastructure destruction in the Gulf of Mexico and onshore Louisiana caused by Hurricane Katrina; a 200 percent or more rise in the price of natural gas in the 2005–2006 winter heating season; and $70 per barrel of oil. Can we expect Congress and federal energy regulators to respond effectively to the energy challenges of the new century? The history of natural gas regulation, where the federal government has long exercised primary regulatory control, is not cause for optimism.

This chapter includes modest proposals for improving the regulatory process and aligning the interests of regulated energy companies with good public policy. The chapter also comments on the need to decode the message the price signals in the energy market are sending and make the hard choices necessary to secure our energy future.

A Short History of the Ambiguous Results of Natural Gas Regulation

Short-sighted regulation combined with poorly conceived and implemented legislation have caused or contributed to periodic natural gas shortages, price swings, catastrophic financial losses for interstate natural gas pipelines, and a less-than-optimum infrastructure. The Natural Gas Act of 1938,[2] along with the Federal Power Act of 1935,[3] were part of the depression-era legislation intended to bring order to what was perceived as industry chaos, destructive competition, and abusive and unsound practices. The FERC's predecessor, the Federal Power Commission (FPC), created (or at least acquiesced in) an industry structure under which interstate natural gas pipelines were financed and constructed based on long-term commitments of natural gas reserves by producers and long-term contracts for the sale and delivery of natural gas to state-regulated local distribution companies

---

[2] 15 U.S.C. § 717 et seq.
[3] 16 U.S.C. § 824 et seq. Congress established the Federal Power Commission in 1920 when it passed legislation to license hydroelectric projects on navigable waterways in the Federal Water Power Act, which is now Title I of the Federal Power Act.

(LDCs) and large industrial end users. For the first fifty years of the modern natural gas industry, pipelines performed the merchant function as the middlemen between the producers and customers. The FPC did not regulate wellhead prices directly. Rather, the FPC reviewed the prices paid by interstate pipelines in setting cost-based rates for the pipelines' sales of gas to local distribution companies.[4]

Notwithstanding occasional complaints about the price of natural gas, this system provided a degree of price stability while allowing the wellhead price of natural gas to be set by market forces. In 1954, however, the U.S. Supreme Court held that the FPC's jurisdiction under the Natural Gas Act extended to independent producers and required the FPC to regulate wellhead sales in interstate commerce.[5] The application of the FPC's licensing and cost-based rate regulation regime to wellhead sales proved disastrous, creating separate interstate and intrastate markets for natural gas. Wellhead price regulation suppressed the supply of gas available to the interstate market due in part to inadequate price levels and the requirement of permanent "dedication" of reserves to interstate commerce.

By the 1970s, severe shortages of natural gas had developed in the interstate market with curtailments of virtually all industrial uses. At the same time, natural gas was plentiful at higher prices in the unregulated intrastate Texas and Louisiana markets, where gas was produced and large petrochemical and industrial uses were located.[6] Rather than address the problem directly through decontrol of the commodity, regulators and government officials encouraged "supplemental" gas projects, including liquefied natural gas (LNG) terminals, construction of an Arctic natural gas pipeline, and high-Btu coal gasification. These projects proved to be boondoggles, providing no real relief from gas shortages and saddling rate-payers and taxpayers with extra costs, although LNG has made resurgence.

---

[4] The Natural Gas Act gave the FPC the authority to regulate the transportation of natural gas and sales for resale in interstate commerce. The FPC did not regulate direct sales of natural gas by pipelines to industrial end users. The allocation of costs to these unregulated sales became a major issue in pipeline rate cases during the first fifty years of regulation. *See generally,* Means & Angyal, *The Regulation and Future Role of Direct Producer Sales,* 5 Energy L.J. 1 (1984).
[5] *Phillips Petroleum Corp. v. Wisconsin,* 347 U.S. 672 (1954).
[6] R. Tussing and C. Barlow, *The Natural Gas Industry: Evolution, Structure and Economics,* 59-60 (1984).

Finally recognizing that NGA-type cost of service regulation of natural gas production was unworkable, Congress passed the Natural Gas Policy Act (NGPA) of 1978, which provided for pricing of existing natural gas by "vintage" (i.e., generally the year the well began producing) and gradual decontrol of new natural gas supplies starting with immediate decontrol of natural gas produced from deep wells below 15,000 feet and various unconventional sources. While well-intentioned, the smooth transition to full deregulation envisioned by the drafters of the NGPA was a pipe dream. Gas-hungry interstate pipelines, who needed additional reserves to meet contractual and regulatory supply obligations and to maintain reserve ratios included in their bond covenants, bid up the price of deregulated reserves to "supra-competitive levels" in the expectation that they would be able to average or "roll-in" the above-market cost of deregulated reserves with the below-natural cost of existing price-controlled gas to deliver a gas steam at marketable prices.[7]

Meanwhile, the natural gas shortage of the 1970s turned into a gas surplus less than five years after passage of the NGPA. The "supra-market" prices paid by pipelines for deregulated gas (up to 130 percent of the Btu-equivalent price of No. 2 fuel oil delivered in New York harbor) incentivized producers to invest in new technology to maximize drilling and production and explore for new reserves at great depths. In addition, gas that previously was bottled up in the intrastate market flowed nationally. Coupled with restrictions on natural gas usage embodied in legislation passed along with the NGPA, fuel-switching by industrial and commercial customers that could use oil or natural gas, and conservation, natural gas pipelines found themselves holding contracts that required them to take or pay for more natural gas than they could sell at prices that were higher than the market was willing to bear. The FERC greatly exacerbated the financial toll on interstate pipelines in mid-1984 by holding on a generic basis that "minimum bill" provisions in the gas sales contracts

---

[7] *See* Williams, *The Proposed Sea-Change in Natural Gas Regulation*, 6 Energy L.J. 233, 237-38 (1985) ("*All* the interstate pipelines bid supra-market prices for gas in 1978-82. A natural question is what would have happened to a pipeline that refused to do so. The answer is—disaster. Any pipeline that limited its bids to true market prices would have found itself short of gas and almost certainly in breach of both contractual and regulatory duties to supply gas. With rolled-in pricing and the NGPA system of wellhead price controls, it was a mathematical *necessity*, for the natural gas market to clear, that some gas be bought at prices above market levels.")

between interstate pipelines and their customers[8] were unjust and unreasonable under the NGA, thereby freeing pipeline customers to buy gas directly from producers and marketers, and make separate arrangements for transportation.

The pipelines, however, still controlled the right to transportation and were not about to provide transportation of gas their sales customers purchased from third parties except where they thought the customer would switch to another pipeline. Therefore, in order to make the gas sales market more competitive, the FERC issued new rules in 1985, which essentially forced interstate pipelines to separate the sales and transportation functions (referred to as "unbundling"), offer transportation service on a non-discriminatory basis to the extent of each pipeline's capacity, and allow their sales customers to convert their sales agreements into transportation contracts so the customers could buy gas from third parties. The FERC followed up with additional "open access" rules in 1992, which gave firm transportation customers quasi-property rights to pipeline capacity similar to leases of real property. Not only could firm capacity holders use their capacity to ship gas, they could also sublease their rights to others on a temporary or permanent basis and subdivide their rights—the transportation equivalent of renting out a whole house or just a room. These actions achieved the FERC's goal of creating a robust, competitive market for natural gas with many buyers and sellers, and the development of futures and options markets, but at enormous transition costs. Producers, pipelines, and their customers spent years in countless court proceedings and before the FERC litigating the issue of who would bear the cost of the above-market, take-or-pay gas purchase contracts that pipelines had entered into. Before the overhang of these contracts was eliminated, pipelines absorbed on the order of $5 billion from take-or-pay settlements, and pipeline customers paid even more.[9] One major pipeline,

---

[8] "Minimum bill" provisions were reciprocal obligations in pipeline-LDC gas sales contracts to the "take or pay" obligations in producer-pipeline gas sales contracts. Pipeline firm sales contracts obligated the pipeline to stand ready to provide a daily contract quantity of gas to the buyer. The minimum bill obligated the buyer to purchase and take a minimum percentage of the daily contract quantity, although the minimum bill calculation was usually based on annual volumes.

[9] Accurate estimates of the cost of resolving the take-or-pay contracts problem are hard to find. One report, prepared by the Energy Information Administration, estimated that, as of May of 1995, pipelines had incurred $10.2 billion of take-or-pay contract settlement costs, of which $6.6 billion was being recovered from consumers.

which faced $13 billion of take-or-pay contract claims from producers, filed for Chapter 11 bankruptcy in 1991 and did not emerge from bankruptcy until 1995.

While deregulation of wellhead prices and the restructuring of the pipeline industry were necessary long-term steps to create an efficient, market-driven industry, poorly thought out legislative and regulatory implementation made the process longer and more expensive than necessary. The resulting faulty price signals, along with improvements in production technology, produced a glut of natural gas by the mid-1980s that was not worked off until 1999–2000. The average sales price of was less than $2 per Mcf in eleven of fourteen years from 1986 to 1999, compared to an average wellhead price of $7.51 per Mcf in 2005. Ironically, as investment capital and human talent moved out of oil and gas exploration and production, the electric industry, which was in the early stages of its own restructuring beginning with the Energy Policy Act of 1992, was looking to natural gas as the fuel of choice for the next generation of electric generating plants because of natural gas's low price, efficiency, and low emissions relative to other fossil fuels. From the mid-1990s into 2004, virtually all new electric generating plants planned and constructed in the United States were gas-fired. While the National Petroleum Council forecasted in 1999 that there would be 113,000 MW of gas-fired electric generation in place by 2010, there was in fact 220,000 MW of gas-fired generation in place by 2004. As the demand from electric generation absorbed the excess supply, the natural gas industry failed to recognize that domestic production of conventional gas was declining, and that imported gas from Canada was meeting most of the incremental demand created by electric generation. Suddenly, in the 2000–2001 winter, the supply/demand balances tightened, natural gas prices tripled, and the country was facing another natural gas crisis.

It is beyond the scope of this chapter to discuss the impact of the collapse of the dot.com boom and its impact on electric demand, the Enron collapse, the energy trading scandals, the collapse of the California experiment with electric restructuring, and the impact on energy infrastructure of Hurricane Katrina in 2005. Suffice it to say that these events stand as a reminder of our collective inability to make accurate macroeconomic forecasts or to detect flaws in the system before they have disastrous consequences. Given the difficulty of recognizing and properly reacting to macroeconomic changes in energy markets, there are regulatory changes that effected energy companies can seek to promote energy efficiency while improving their profit picture (doing well by doing good) and that will increase their willingness to invest in new infrastructure projects.

Representing Regulated Natural Gas Pipelines and Local Distribution Companies in a Changing Regulatory and Supply/Demand Environment: A Modest Agenda

The transformation of interstate pipelines from sellers of natural gas to transporters of gas owned by third parties created a competitive market with many sellers and buyers of the commodity and an embryonic market for pipeline capacity. However, residential and small commercial customers, and to a lesser degree, large industrial customers and municipalities, still needed some entity to perform the "aggregation" function and ensure reliable delivery of the product. This function, and overall gas supply management for most customers, has largely fallen on the shoulders of the nation's local distribution companies along with third-party marketer/aggregators, and has provided new challenges for their attorneys, who must draft and review contracts for the sales of gas and of pipeline capacity. A voluntary standards-setting organization, known as the North American Energy Standards Board (NAESB), has developed a model natural gas sales contract, which most buyers and sellers use as a starting point for their transactions. The parties then negotiate "special provisions," which have grown more elaborate over the last five years. The Base Contract is available for purchase on the NAESB Web site, www.naesb.org. The Edison Electric Institute, which is the primary trade association for U.S. shareholder-owned electric companies, publishes a similar model contract for the sale of electricity.

In light of the turbulent fifty-year history of energy regulation and the volatility of energy prices, energy regulatory lawyers add value where they can align the interests of their clients with outcomes that would be good public policy. A significant portion of my practice consists of representing companies in the business of transporting and delivering natural gas to consumers and whose rates, business practices, and profit are regulated at the federal level by the FERC or at the state level by state public utility commissions. Like other businesses, regulated companies respond to price incentives. Unfortunately, the incentives created by cost of service rate-making historically used by the FERC and most state public utility commissions do not promote efficiency. The profit earned by the regulated company is a function of the company's investment in pipe in the ground and the other facilities and equipment required to provide the service on which the company earns a rate of return. The company cannot grow its profit consistently without making more investment. Further, because the company's investment base (referred to as the "rate base") declines with depreciation, the regulated company needs to continue investing in new plant in order to maintain its existing level of profitability. This creates a climate where the focus is on the most investment rather than the best investment. In fact, the process discourages efficiency gains by requiring the regulated entity to reduce its rates periodically to reflect cost savings. A client's interests can be aligned with good policy by proposing to regulators that they provide incentives to encourage more efficient investment and operation, for example, by allowing the regulated company to retain a significant portion of the efficiency gains permanently or for a period of years beyond the next rate review. Similarly, counsel can advocate to regulators that they should permit higher rates of return for investments that increase efficiency, such as replacing old technology or adding computer systems that allow the pipeline to optimize gas flows and provide more transportation service with the same pipeline facilities.

Energy regulatory attorneys also can align the interests of their clients with good policy by convincing regulators to adopt rate structures that encourage the regulated company to promote conservation and efficient utilization of natural gas by customers. Most LDC rates are designed so the non-gas costs of providing service, including the return on the LDC's investment (the profit component), are recovered volumetrically based on forecast deliveries to end users (i.e., sales and transportation throughput).[10] Likewise, under traditional rate designs, the fixed costs of the distribution of electricity are recovered volumetrically based on a forecast of kilowatt

---

[10] Most local distribution companies do not earn a profit on the natural gas they sell to customers. Rather, the gas rates are designed as a cost pass-through with adjustments for under- or over-collection of gas costs.

hours sold.[11] Under these conditions, a reduction in the deliveries of natural gas or electricity to customers due to successful energy efficiency and conservation programs reduces the utility's earnings. While utilities in this position may make some limited effort to promote energy efficiency for image purposes, such as weatherization programs for low-income consumers, they will not invest in comprehensive and sustained end-use efficiency and conservation programs.

It is possible, however, to eliminate the disincentive for utilities to invest in end-use energy efficiency by "decoupling" the direct connection between utility sales and earnings. Decoupling can be accomplished by recovering more fixed costs in monthly customer demand charges, using rate "true-ups," and allowing utilities to share in the cost savings from well-designed energy efficiency programs. The Natural Resources Defense Council and the American Gas Association support decoupling, and several states are currently looking at decoupling. The Oregon Public Utility Commission and utilities in Oregon have been at the forefront in implementing decoupling through the use of deferred accounts, which adjust revenues for changes in per-customer usage, and the establishment of an independent energy trust funded by the utilities, which makes investments that improve energy efficiency. Detailed information on the Oregon approach can be obtained from the author or the Oregon Public Utility Commission. Investing in energy efficiency can become an integral part of the corporate culture of utilities if the right incentives are created.

Finally, it is time to reexamine the risks of investments in energy infrastructure and the manner in which regulators structure financial returns to regulated companies. Regulators need to recognize that investments in energy infrastructure are becoming riskier, particularly for investments in infrastructure for the transmission and distribution of natural gas, since it is becoming clearer that the United States alone and in combination with Canada cannot meet U.S. demand for natural gas, and the country is becoming increasingly reliant on less secure foreign sources. Domestic production of natural gas peaked in 1973 at

---

[11] If the utility owns its own generation facilities, the allowed return on that investment will also be reflected in the utility's rates, and the cost of fuel burned to produce the power will be a pass-through. If the utility has contracted for power from independent generators, the cost of that power will be reflected in the utility's rates at the contract cost.

approximately 62 billion cubic feet (Bcf) per day. Domestic production is struggling today to stay in the 50 to 55 Bcf per day range despite a dramatic increase in wellhead prices, large annual increases in drilling activity each year since the 2000–2001 winter, and the development of "unconventional" supplies such as coal bed methane. The decline rates in existing fields appear to be outpacing the discovery and development of new prospects, especially with the offshore Atlantic and Pacific coasts off-limits to new drilling. For over fifteen years, secure Canadian supplies have offset the shortfall in domestic gas production, but Canadian supply peaked in 2001 and 2002. With Canada unable to increase its exports above existing levels, the United States has turned to LNG imports. However, the ability of LNG to meet U.S. demand is open to question. An LNG liquefaction plant capable of producing 390 Bcf of LNG per year (approximately five days' worth of U.S. demand) requires $1.5 to $2.0 billion of capital investment, plus the investment in LNG tankers and the construction of LNG receiving terminals. Suffice it to say, there are material financial and environmental barriers to increasing LNG sufficiently to meet U.S. demand.

Given this new reality concerning natural gas supply, the FERC and state utility commissions should take a more sophisticated approach to rate-setting in order to encourage sufficient investment in energy infrastructure. Regulators need to examine return on capital (allowed earnings), return of capital (depreciation), and rate design jointly to determine the cash flows necessary to create a robust investment environment that still protects consumers from excessive rates. Under the current rate-making approach of the FERC and many state public utility commissions, rate of return, depreciation, and rate design are viewed as separate components in the rate-making process. Many interstate pipelines have mainline depreciation rates under 2.0 percent, which imply a capital recovery period of more than fifty years. These existing depreciation rates tend to be used in setting rates for new projects by existing pipelines. Using a depreciation rate of 2.0 percent, 50 percent of the investment made in a project today will be returned to the utility twenty-six to fifty years from now. It should be obvious that the present value of the cash flow from depreciation in year twenty-six and beyond is near zero.[12] Given the uncertainties associated with the future of

---

[12] At a discount rate of 8 percent, the present value of an investment of $100 returned over fifty years at 2 percent depreciation is $13.42.

supply and the importance of having a robust infrastructure capable of meeting peak demand, it is reasonable for regulators to allow regulated companies to recover their capital investment over much shorter time periods and to evaluate the impact of accelerated cost recovery in setting rates of return. In addition, the return on capital and the return of capital should be levelized so customers are not burdened with front-end-loaded rates.[13]

The proposals set forth above, standing alone, can do little more than make a modest contribution toward improving energy supply and reducing demand; but they do set a tone of recognizing that the country has serious energy problems and acting in an economically sophisticated manner to address them.

Are Policymakers Missing the Message the Energy Markets Are Sending? Major Changes in Energy Policy Are Needed to Ensure Our Energy Future

As this chapter is being written, crude oil is trading between $70 and $75 per barrel, the "spot" price of natural gas is near $7 per MMBtu, the "forward" price for the 2006–2007 winter heating season is in the $11 per MMBtu range, and regular unleaded gasoline is in excess of $3 per gallon at the pump. The major oil companies are reporting record profits, the public wants lower prices, and politicians are looking for someone to blame. What the country does not have and what politicians are not talking about is a balanced, overall energy strategy that requires real change in consumer behavior. EPACT 2005 overall was a positive step, but a small one. The legislation is a series of incremental actions that focus heavily on tax incentives and subsidies. EPACT 2005 does not reflect any sense of urgency and does not make any hard choices.

The soaring prices of oil and natural gas suggest the need for urgency. It is now clear that surging demand has absorbed the oil and natural gas supply

---

[13] The front-end load problem occurs under depreciated original cost rate-making with "straight line" depreciation because the regulated company's earnings on a new investment are bunched into the early years when before straight-line depreciation reduces the net book value of the investment. Levelizing the return and depreciation eliminates this problem.

cushion of the 1990s. The Energy Information Administration, the International Energy Agency, and other forecasters conservatively estimate that demand for oil will grow by 50 percent between now and 2020 to 2030 from 80 million to 120 million barrels a day. The worldwide demand growth for natural gas is forecast to be even greater. Given the surge in demand in China, India, and other developing countries, these forecasts of demand growth could be too low. Where will the increased supply come from to meet this demand growth? Non-OPEC supplies of oil are peaking. Despite large increases in drilling in the last five years, non-OPEC oil production has been flat except for some growth in production from the countries of the former Soviet Union. Total non-OPEC production was approximately 49 million bbl/d in 2005, with the difference of 30 to 35 million bbl/d provided by OPEC. The ability of OPEC (and, in particular, Saudi Arabia) to double existing production over fifteen to twenty-five years is very much in doubt. A startling fact is that there have not been any discoveries of major new oil fields in the Middle East since 1968 and elsewhere in the world since 1972. Putting aside the national security issues associated with increased reliance on energy supplies from the Middle East and the former Soviet Union, the United States cannot afford to assume that higher prices will elicit the necessary supply and demand response without volatility and crisis.

Under the circumstances, the United States needs to design *and implement* a meaningful, balanced energy strategy—a Marshall Plan for energy—rather than produce a document that gathers dust on the shelf or is the subject of endless debate. The elements of the policy should include: (1) mandatory energy efficiency measures, including mandatory appliance efficiency standards, an increase in the Corporate Average Fuel Economy Standards and the closing of loopholes in that program so all vehicle classes are included, and increased emphasis on demand side management; (2) undertaking a comprehensive field-by-field energy audit of proven and probable energy reserves, decline rates, and related information based on testing (to the extent possible, this should be international and should be considered a national security priority); (3) relaxing or removing the ban on offshore drilling (unlike Arctic reserves, offshore Atlantic and Pacific coast reserves can be attached to the energy delivery network relatively inexpensively, assuming the existence of commercially viable reserves); (4) greatly increased support for research on renewable energy and energy efficiency technologies; (5) accelerated development of nuclear power; and (6) increased taxes on gasoline with tax credits to low- and middle-income taxpayers to offset the impact of energy taxes.

As a nation, we can absorb a little pain now to avoid severe injury to our energy future.

Jeff Komarow has a diverse litigation and counseling practice primarily focused on federal regulation of energy and the construction of energy and other projects. He is known for developing innovative strategies and is frequently asked to take on difficult and complex regulatory and commercial issues.

Mr. Komarow represents clients in litigation and rule-makings before the Federal Energy Regulatory Commission, in related court appeals, and in commercial negotiations involving energy projects and the sale and transportation of natural gas and electricity. In addition, working closely with other members of the construction and procurement group, Mr. Komarow represents owners and contractors in arbitrations and court litigation involving the construction of power plants, natural gas facilities, and other large-scale projects.

Previously, Mr. Komarow was an articles editor of the Michigan Law Review, *law clerk to the late Judge Edward A. Tamm pf the U.S. Court of Appeals for the District of Columbia Circuit, and, for eighteen years, a member of a Washington, D.C., law firm that specializes in energy law.*

Mr. Komarow is in his second term as chair of the citizens committee that advises the county executive and Council of Montgomery County, Maryland, on energy and air quality matters.

Dedication: *To Sandi, for whose love and support I am eternally grateful.*

Appendices

CONTENTS

Appendix A: Request for Clarification and/or Rehearing   144

Appendix B: Pro-Company License with a University   174

Appendix C: Agreement to Release Interstate Pipeline Capacity and Firm Transportation Contract Rights   202

APPENDIX A

UNITED STATES OF AMERICA
BEFORE THE
FEDERAL ENERGY REGULATORY COMMISSION

Transactions Subject to FPA Section 203   Docket No. RM05-34-000

REQUEST FOR CLARIFICATION AND/OR REHEARING OF BANK OF AMERICA, N.A. AND JPMORGAN CHASE BANK, N.A.

Bank of America, N.A. (BofA) and JPMorgan Chase Bank, N.A. (JPMCB) respectfully request rehearing and/or clarification of the Commission's regulations respecting transactions subject to Section 203 of the Federal Power Act (FPA), as amended by the Energy Policy Act of 2005 (EPAct 2005).[1]

BofA is a national banking association and member of the Federal Reserve System. The principal business of BofA is commercial banking and financial services. BofA is a wholly-owned subsidiary of Bank of America Corp., a Delaware corporation, a bank holding company and a financial holding company under the Gramm-Leach-Bliley Act. Directly and through its various subsidiaries, Bank of America Corp. provides a diversified and comprehensive range of commercial and investment banking and nonbanking financial services and products (including deposit-taking and other funds generation, corporate, mortgage and consumer lending, corporate advisory services, brokerage, fund management, and intermediation of transactions in all types of financial instruments) throughout the United States and in selected international markets.

JPMCB is a national banking association and member of the Federal Reserve System. Its parent, JPMorgan Chase & Co., is a financial holding company incorporated under Delaware law. JPMorgan Chase & Co. is a leading global financial services firm with assets of $1.2 trillion and

---

[1] Final Rule re Transactions Subject to FPA Section 203, 113 FERC 61,315 (2005) ("Order No. 669").

operations in more than 50 countries. The firm is a leader in investment banking, financial services for consumers and businesses, financial transaction processing, asset and wealth management, and private equity.

I. INTRODUCTION AND STATEMENT OF ISSUES

In its current form, and depending on how it is interpreted, Order No. 669 could have a significant adverse impact on the routine investments of banks and their related financial entities within Regulated Banking Groups.[2] Many such transactions would become newly subject to FPA Section 203 approval if such Groups are treated as "holding companies" and their routine acquisitions of utility securities are made subject to Federal Energy Regulatory Commission (FERC or the Commission) pre-acquisition approval requirements.

Acquisitions of utility securities interests in fiduciary capacities typically have a short time frame that cannot await the outcome of the approval process. Thus, imposition of a pre-acquisition approval requirement would disrupt Banks' implementation of fiduciary obligations, impair their financing of the utility sector, and discourage them from participating in the utility sector as power marketers and investors in wholesale generation. Such an outcome could not have been contemplated by Congress, which enacted a special exclusion from the definition of "holding company" in EPAct 2005 for banks and broker-dealers. Such an outcome would also be inconsistent with the relief that the Commission previously granted to bank power marketers under the acquisition clause of Section 203(a)(1). This specially tailored relief was granted in recognition that bank investments in utilities in the ordinary course of their business are already regulated by banking authorities.

---

[2] The Regulated Banking Groups to which this Request for Clarification and/or Rehearing is intended to apply consist of: (i) banks chartered and regulated under the laws of the United States or a U.S. state, and (ii) bank holding companies registered as such with (and subject to supervision and regulation by) the Federal Reserve Board under the Bank Holding Company Act of 1956 (as amended by the Gramm-Leach-Bliley Act of 1999 (GLB Act), the BHC Act), in each case together with their subsidiaries.

145

BofA and JPMCB believe that the adverse effect of Order No. 669 was unintended and that clarification of Order No. 669, the blanket authorization process, or other procedural avenues may be available to mitigate these severe but unintended consequences. BofA and JPMCB identify the following issues:

(i) *Clarification that Statutorily Exempt Interests Are Not Aggregated with Nonexempt Interests for Purposes of the 10% Thresholds in the Definition of "Holding Company" and in FERC's Blanket Authorization.* Under EPAct 2005, "holding company" is defined as a company that holds 10% or more of the voting securities of a public utility company or holding company. Order No. 669 grants blanket authorization for investors to hold up to 10% of the voting securities. Congress has determined, however, that bank holdings of utility securities in a fiduciary capacity, as collateral, or in connection with the liquidation of a loan, as well as certain broker-dealer investments, should be excluded from the definition of "holding company." The Commission should clarify that statutorily-exempted holdings by banks and broker-dealers are not to be aggregated with other holdings by non-exempt entities in the same Regulated Banking Group for purposes of applying to such non-exempt entities the 10% thresholds in the definition of "holding company" and in FERC's blanket authorization. The Commission should avoid penalizing nonexempt bank investments because such investments might be foreclosed where, for example, the exempt fiduciary holdings of a bank in the same Regulated Banking Group approach or exceed 10%. Attributing bank exempt holdings in a given utility's securities to nonexempt entities in the same Regulated Banking Group would defeat the Congressional intent to exclude fiduciary and loan-related holdings from coverage under FERC holding company regulation.

(ii) *Clarification of Exclusion or Blanket Authorization of Fiduciary Investments.* Investments in a fiduciary capacity by financial institutions in a Regulated Banking Group are subject to a stringent regime overseen by U.S. bank regulators and do not raise issues of control over public utilities. The Commission should clarify that investments by such financial institutions in a fiduciary capacity should be excluded from the scope of Section 203(a)(2) or, in the alternative, should grant such fiduciary investments blanket authorization.

(iii) *Confirmation that Relief from the "Acquisition of Securities" Clause under Section 203 (a) (1) Applies under Section 203 (a) (2).* FERC has previously granted many banks that function as power marketers relief from the "acquisition of securities" clause in Section 203(a)(1). For example, such banks need not seek pre-approval from FERC where they acquire utility securities in debt, fiduciary, trading, or hedging capacities. Banks have received such relief based on Commission recognition of the role of regulators in supervising banks and the importance as a policy matter of allowing bank investments in utility securities. However, a bank now could be separately subject to newly-enacted Section 203(a)(2) as a "holding company." The Commission should clarify that the same relief applies under Section 203(a)(2), subject to the same conditions, as is applied under Section 203(a)(1).

(iv) *Exclusion of or Blanket Authorization for Companies Which Are Only "Holding Companies" by Virtue of QF/EWG Ownership from Section 203 (a) (2).* BofA and JPMCB join many other commenters in concluding that the Commission erred in finding that holding exempt wholesale generators (EWGs) and qualifying facilities (QFs) should subject a company to "holding company" status and, thus, to pre-acquisition review under Section 203(a)(2). BofA and JPMCB therefore join in the request that FERC grant rehearing and/or provide blanket authorization for such holdings subject to appropriate conditions and safeguards where companies would only be "holding companies" by virtue of their ownership of interests in QFs or EWGs.

II. RECOGNIZING THEIR STRINGENT REGULATORY REGIME AND SPECIAL ROLE IN THE FINANCIAL MARKETPLACE, CONGRESS AND FERC HAVE ACCORDED SPECIAL AUTHORIZATIONS TO BANKING GROUPS

Congress, in the definition of "holding company," and the Commission, in its market-based rate orders issued to bank power marketers, have granted exclusions and authorizations to banks in Regulated Banking Groups. These actions recognize the need to enable financial institutions to participate in debt and equity investments to public utilities and the special character of such investments when made by financial institutions. These actions also recognize the existence of a sophisticated bank regulatory regime that mitigates any concern that acquisition of securities by banks could be misused as a vehicle to acquire control of utility securities without the oversight of FERC.

Although both Congress and FERC share a common purpose to enable banks and related financial institutions to continue their normal and critically important fiduciary and investment activities, Order No. 669 does not fully achieve this result. In part these issues of interpretation and implementation arise because EPAct 2005 did not address all of the issues previously considered by the Commission in its market-based rate orders issued to bank power marketers. In part, these issues might arise because FERC is not fully aware of the full scope of fiduciary and investment activities conducted by other bank-affiliated entities in the same Regulated Banking Group.

BofA and JPMCB request that the Commission revisit certain aspects of Order No. 669, and issue blanket authorizations, clarifications, or other relief as appropriate, to mitigate the apparently unintended consequences of Order No. 669 on financial institutions in Regulated Banking Groups and to fully effectuate Congressional intent and FERC's prior decisions.

A.   **Bank and Broker-Dealer Exclusion under EPAct 2005**

A statutory exemption for "banks" under EPAct 2005 excludes banks and bank operating subsidiaries from the definition of "holding company" where banks "own, control, or hold, with the power to vote, public utility or public utility holding company securities so long as the securities are- (I) held as collateral for a loan; (II) held in the ordinary course of business as a fiduciary; or (III) acquired solely for purposes of liquidation and in connection with a loan previously contracted for and owned beneficially for a period of not more than 2 years." EPAct 2005 § 1 262(8)(B)(i). A broker-

APPENDICES

dealer is exempt if its holdings are "(I) not beneficially owned by the broker or dealer and are subject to any voting instructions which may be given by the customers or their assigns; or (II) acquired within 12 months in the ordinary course of business as a broker, dealer or underwriter with the bona fide intention of effecting distribution of the specific securities so acquired." Id. § 1262(8)(B)(ii).

These exclusions raise to a statutory level, and expand upon, the regulatory exemptions, known as Rule 3 and Rule 4, that had been issued by the Securities and Exchange Commission (SEC) under the Public Utility Holding Act of 1935 (PUHCA 1935) and evidence Congressional intent to exclude financial institution investments from the ambit of the Section 203(a)(2) approval process. Far from seeking to burden financial institutions with new obligations, EPAct 2005 provides statutory exemptions for banks and broker-dealers from the definition of "holding company." While these definitions specifically address fiduciary and loan-related holdings and holdings acquired for the purpose of liquidating a debt, a fair reading of these exemptions is that Congress intended to avoid any impediment to the participation by banking organizations in the utility sector as lender or investor. While many of the Bank Regulated Group's holdings will fall within the four corners of the statutory exemption, they will not all be exempt under the "bank" or "broker-dealer" exemption since they also conducts fiduciary or lending activities in other entities in the same Regulated Banking Group where such entities are not themselves broker-dealers, banks or operating subsidiaries of banks (even though, as discussed below, the Regulated Banking Groups are subject to U.S. bank regulatory supervision).

B. Bank Power Marketer Authorizations Issued by the Commission

The Commission first considered at great length the need to exclude bank investments from Section 203(a) approval in the UBS/Bank of America proceeding. After a multi-stage process that took account of the nature of the investments, the regulatory regime to which the applicant bank power marketers are subject, and the purposes of Section 203 review, the Commission granted a series of specific authorizations for particular types of investments. The Commission has granted the same authorizations to other banks in subsequent orders. Under these precedents, for a bank power marketer, the following authorizations apply:

   a. Bank power marketers utilities may own up to 5% of voting equity securities as principal of each voting class of securities issued by a utility (provided that the bank power marketer obtains no right to control the operation or management of the utility).
   b. Debt securities and dealer/trader activities are excluded from the 5% limit on holdings as principal.
   c. Fiduciary holdings are excluded from the 5% limit on holdings as principal.
   d. Acquisition of utility securities in connection with underwritings is not subject to the 5% limit on holdings as principal. This exemption automatically extends for 45 days; in the case of failed underwritings, the exemption is extended if the bank files within 45 days for Section 203 approval to retain the securities and commits not to vote the securities held as a result of the failed underwriting.
   e. Where bank regulators allow bank power marketers to hold more than 5% of voting equity securities of a utility as principal for derivatives hedging purposes (under "safety and soundness" principles), the 5% limit on holdings as principal may be exceeded based on a commitment not to vote securities in question.
   f. Bank power marketers and their affiliates must report by public utility (i) their holdings of voting equity securities held as principal and (ii) their total holdings of voting equity securities irrespective of the capacity in which such securities are held within 45 days of the close of each calendar quarter. The reports are subject to a de minimis threshold of 1%.

UBS AG and Bank of America N.A., 101 FERC 61,312 (2002), reh 'g granted in part and denied in part, 103 FERC 61,284 (2003), reh. granted, 105 FERC 61,078 (2003); JPMorgan Chase Bank, N.A., Docket No. ER05-283 (letter order dated March 18, 2005).

BofA and JPMCB respectfully request that FERC now assure that the same relief is fully applicable under the newly-expanded scope of Section 203 review (and, in particular, in respect of the holding company approvals required under Section 203(a)(2)). In seeking clarification or other relief as set out below, we further note that: (i) the Commission will have full information about the holdings of public utility interests, as pursuant to their bank power marketer orders the Regulated Bank Groups are required to report their voting security investments subject to a de minimis threshold of 1%; and (ii) apart from the relief previously granted to bank power marketers, any of their other affiliates that are public utilities within the meaning of FPA Section 201(e) would continue to be subject to the acquisition of securities clause of Section 203 (a)(1).

III. THE COMMISSION SHOULD CLARIFY THAT STATUTORILY EXCLUDED BANK AND BROKER-DEALER HOLDINGS SHOULD NOT BE AGGREGATED WITH OTHER HOLDINGS OF NONEXEMPT ENTITIES IN THE SAME REGULATED BANKING GROUP

BofA and JPMCB request clarification that, as is contemplated by the statute and supported by policy and FERC precedent, the interests of exempt and nonexempt affiliates would not be aggregated for purposes of applying the 10% thresholds applicable to both the definition of holding company, EPAct 2005 § 1262(8), and the blanket authorization granted by Order No. 669 under Section 203(a)(2). 18 C.F.R. § 33.1(c)(2).

The starting point for analysis is the text of the statute. As discussed above, Section 1262(8) of EPAct 2005 states that "the term 'holding company' shall not include" banks and operating subsidiaries and broker-dealers whose holdings of securities meet certain conditions. Further, the definition of "holding company system" is "a holding company, together with its subsidiary companies." EPAct 2005 § 1262(9). Accordingly, this situation is different from that under PUHCA 1935 and SEC Rule 3, where banks could fall within the definition of holding company but were by rule excluded from its obligations.[3] By contrast, under EPAct 2005, banks and

---

[3] Although not directly relevant here, we note that the under PUHCA 1935, the SEC briefly considered, but never decided, the issue of aggregation where financial institutions hold interests in public utilities. Fidelity, Release No. 35-26448 (Jan. 5, 1996), 1996 SEC LEXIS 109. The voting securities of reorganized El Paso Electric were held by approximately twenty-one separate Fidelity funds and accounts, none of which would hold an amount equal to 10% or more. The Commission noted that "[u]nless these interests are aggregated, Fidelity is not a holding company

their operating subsidiaries are excluded from the definition of holding company itself, to the extent that their utility holdings are in loan-related or fiduciary capacities. Aggregation of nonexempt holdings with excluded holdings would directly contravene the statutory language.

The Congressional elevation of the bank exclusion to statutory status reinforces the importance of the underlying policies to assure liquidity in the utility industry by allowing banks to hold utility interests in fiduciary and specified loan capacities without being considered holding companies. Full implementation of the exclusion is necessary to effectuate legislative intent.

Counting exempt utility holdings by banks and their operating subsidiaries toward the 10% threshold would have the perverse result of disadvantaging non-bank affiliates of exempt entities vis-à-vis their similarly situated competitors because exempt interests of exempt entities and their subsidiaries could swallow the 10% allowance. In other words, a non-bank entity in a Regulated Banking Group might be foreclosed from acquiring utility interests in a utility where an exempt bank and its operating subsidiaries in the same Banking Group have extensive (but exempt) holdings in a fiduciary capacity—contrary to the 10% blanket authorization that FERC adopted to promote institutional investment in the utility sector. Moreover, no regulatory purpose would appear to be served by aggregation. To the extent that the interests to be aggregated are those held by sibling companies, these companies would not (by definition) own or control the exempt bank, whose holdings Congress has chosen to exempt.

The purpose of FERC pre-approval also should be considered. FERC has historically been charged with overseeing acquisition, sale, and merger of utility interests—acquisitions that it approves under a regulatory regime designed to assess whether the acquisition increases market power. FERC has stated that it will exercise its new authority over acquisitions by utilities of holding companies under its pre-existing guidelines for review of utility

---

within the meaning of section 2(a)(7) of the Act" and that it "ha[d] not previously addressed the circumstances in which utility interests owned, managed or with respect to which voting power is held, by a company such as Fidelity should be aggregated." However, the SEC did not rule on the aggregation issue because Fidelity requested designation as a holding company exempt from PUHCA 1935, rather than a declaration that it was not a holding company at all.

acquisitions. The focus of that review is market power and protection of jurisdictional (wholesale) ratepayers. The statutory objective is no longer the PUHCA 1935 objective of prohibiting any holding of a utility by entities not engaged in the utility business. In other words, PUHCA 1935 sought to discourage ownership of public utilities in excess of 10% of voting securities. EPAct 2005 seeks to assure that FERC can vet such acquisitions to be sure that they do not increase market power.

There would be no reason to penalize the nonexempt holdings of Regulated Banking Groups when all other non-exempt investors can acquire up to 10% of the voting securities in a utility without being subject to the FERC pre-approval requirement of Section 203(a)(2). In fact, the nonexempt holdings of Regulated Banking Groups are fundamentally passive holdings and fiduciary in nature—inherently not susceptible to exercise of market power.

As explained below, fiduciary holdings by asset management entities within Regulated Banking Groups are subject to bank regulatory and securities regulatory safeguards. The assets must be managed in the interest of the beneficiary, not of the Banking Group. The Federal Reserve Board—the primary regulator of U.S. bank holding companies—affirms the responsibility of fiduciary entities within Regulated Banking Groups to discharge a "fiduciary's duty of undivided loyalty to the trust beneficiaries."[4]

Moreover, the asset management holdings by Regulated Banking Groups should be considered to be passive investor holdings. This is analogous to Shaw Plasma Power (discussed below) where the Commission disclaimed jurisdiction over passive owners who did not own or operate jurisdictional facilities, and had no rights to direct, manage, or control the day-to-day operations of Plasma Power. Similarly, the Commission has interpreted the concept of "control" under Section 203 to be linked to decision-making authority and dominion over the operation of jurisdictional facilities.[5]

Accordingly, to effectuate the statutory exclusion from the definition of holding company and its underlying policy rationale, the exempt holdings of

---

[4] Federal Reserve Board Supervisory Letter No. SR 96-10(SPE), Apr. 24, 1996.
[5] Enova, 79 FERC 61,107 (1997); Central Pacific, 42 FERC 61,073 (1988).

banks, operating subsidiaries and broker-dealers should not to be aggregated with non-exempt holdings for purposes of applying the 10% threshold in the blanket authorization for holdings of voting equity established under Order No. 669. Although the statutory scheme is clear, it does not explicitly address aggregation, and the Commission should issue a clarification to this effect to provide certainty for the regulated community.

IV. FIDUCIARY INVESTMENTS BY FINANCIAL INSTITUTIONS IN A REGULATED BANKING GROUP SHOULD BE EXCLUDED FROM SECTION 203(a)(2) PRIOR APPROVAL

BofA and JPMCB seek a determination that fiduciary investments by their non-bank financial institutions are excluded from the scope of Section 203(a)(2) or in the alternative request blanket authorization for such fiduciary investments. Although fiduciary investments directly by banks and their operating subsidiaries have the benefit of a statutory exclusion, many banks have sibling companies providing nonbank financial services as part of a common banking group. Relief is necessary because it would not be feasible for nonbank fiduciaries to obtain Section 203(a)(2) approval prior to such investments and is appropriate because such investments do not raise issues of control and are subject to stringent regulation under the banking and securities laws. The Commission has previously recognized the special nature of fiduciary investments, granting broad blanket authorizations while tightly limiting principal investments. Because these holdings of non-bank affiliates of banks are similar in nature and are subject to a similar regulatory regime to those made by the bank itself, they also should have the benefit of a Section 203(a)(2) exclusion.

A. Relief Is Necessary to Enable Non-Bank Affiliates to Conduct Their Permissible Investment Activities

Many Regulated Banking Groups, including those of BofA and JPMCB, have non-bank subsidiaries that are continually involved in the routine acquisition and disposition of equity and debt positions in utility securities in fiduciary capacities. These fiduciary relationships are numerous and broad-ranging. They encompass, among other roles, the function of trustee, agent, executor, administrator, guardian, asset manager, discretionary investment adviser and similar capacities. Often these passive interests are transitory, fluctuate frequently, and are undertaken with a short lead-time in the ordinary course of managing a diverse portfolio of investments. These investments are not made for the purpose of permitting the Banking Group to exercise control over the operations of the issuer—indeed they could not, since a fiduciary has an obligation to manage the holdings in the interest of the person on whose behalf the securities are held—and they are already regulated by the comprehensive set of federal and state regimes applicable to financial institutions.

The trading of utility securities and capital investment in utilities would be considerably hampered if Section 203(a) were to apply to such fiduciary holdings, as it would not be feasible to obtain Commission pre-approval in the short time frame in which investment decisions must be made. The imposition of any limits on fiduciary holdings in a Regulated Banking Group would fail to recognize that large, complex global financial service providers act as fiduciary in a wide range of different capacities entirely unrelated to any attempt to acquire or exercise control of the companies whose investments are so held. They typically relate to literally tens of thousands of clients worldwide. Order No. 669's blanket authorization of the acquisition of up to 10% of voting equity of utilities does not provide adequate relief, since on an aggregate basis all holdings in a fiduciary and/or proprietary capacity under a large banking group may in the ordinary course of business approach or exceed the 10% threshold. Subjecting fiduciary holdings of voting equity securities of a public utility by a Regulated Banking Group to a 10% limitation could interfere significantly with the proper functioning of a fiduciary. An institution could be put in the untenable position of having to limit the securities its fiduciary customers could place in trust and similar accounts, or of having to restrict (or restructure) existing or prospective fiduciary relationships.

B. **Fiduciary Investments of Non-Bank Subsidiaries in Regulated Banking Groups are Subject to Oversight under Banking and Securities Laws**

U.S. federal banking laws distinguish between proprietary and fiduciary holdings of securities of U.S. issuers by Regulated Banking Groups, limiting proprietary holdings of such Groups while authorizing fiduciary holdings subject to regulation to prevent self-dealing. The analysis of the U.S. bank regulators is instructive, and their regulatory oversight provides assurance that fiduciary holdings will not raise the control issues that are within the Commission's ambit under Section 203(a).

1. **Distinction Between Proprietary and Fiduciary Holdings Drawn by U.S. Banking Laws**

U.S. federal banking laws draw a clear distinction between proprietary and fiduciary holdings. Congress has historically been very sensitive to assuring that Regulated Banking Groups not become impermissibly involved with U.S. commercial enterprises,[6] and the Federal Reserve Board has consistently maintained that one of the "fundamental purposes of the BHC Act [is] to maintain the separation of banking and commerce."[7] However, as a matter of U.S. federal banking law, Congress has not imposed any specific percentage limitation on the proportion of shares in a particular U.S. non-banking entity that a Regulated Banking Group may hold with discretionary voting rights in a fiduciary capacity on behalf of a third party.[8] BofA and JPMCB submit that the Commission should respect the distinction made in the banking law in the context of holdings of securities of public utilities in a fiduciary capacity, and that such an action on the part of the Commission would be fully consistent with the applicable policies behind the "acquisition-of-securities clause" of Section 203.

2. **Regulation of Fiduciary Holdings under U.S. and Non-U.S. Banking and Securities Laws**

The comprehensive statutory and regulatory regime applicable to financial institutions' fiduciary activities constrain their ability to employ any securities held in a fiduciary capacity so as to benefit themselves or their

---

[6] See, e.g., S. Rep. No. 84-1095 (1955), 1956 U.S. C.C.A.N. 2482, 2484 (the BHC Act is based on the philosophy that bank holding companies should not "manage or control non-banking assets"); S. Rep. No. 106-44 (1999) at 21 (the amendments to the BHC Act effected by the GLB Act, P.L. 106-102, 13 Stat. 1338 (1999) "continu[e] to be attentive not to allow the general mixing of banking and commerce").

[7] 66 Fed. Reg. 8466 (Jan. 31, 2001).

[8] See 12 U.S.C. § 1843(c)(4); 12 C.F.R. § 225.2(d)(3).

affiliates. The Federal Reserve Board—the primary regulator of U.S. bank holding companies—has made clear, for example, that "fiduciary examinations have traditionally focused on risks associated with compliance, financial management and operations, and the fiduciary's duty of undivided loyalty to the trust beneficiaries."[9] This "duty of loyalty" is a pervasive one. As the Federal Reserve Board has stated:

Trustees are obligated to make all decisions based exclusively on the best interests of trust customers. Except as permitted by law, trustees cannot place themselves in a position in which their interests might conflict with those of the trust beneficiaries.[10]

Fiduciary activities—even those conducted outside of a U.S. commercial bank (whether through an investment adviser, hedge fund manager, non-bank trust operation or otherwise)—are subject to significant U.S. statutory and regulatory controls that relate to such matters as the nature of beneficial ownership, the decision-making processes used for selection, retention and preservation of discretionary investments, conflict of interest management, requirements to act in the best interests of an account and treat accounts impartially, requirements to establish procedures and practices designed to prevent conflicts of interest, self-dealing and use of confidential banking or other inside information in making investment decisions, and similar matters. In meeting fiduciary obligations, discretionary decisions must be fit to the nature, purpose and intent of a particular fiduciary relationship and to the statutory framework surrounding that relationship, taking into account the beneficiary's income, assets, risk tolerance, investment objectives, status and the like. For example, in conducting its fiduciary business, the fiduciary must exercise an independent evaluation of the effect, if any, a proposal could have on the current or future value of the investment of the beneficiary, and must vote proxies in a manner consistent with the best interest of the beneficiary.

The SEC also regulates certain fiduciary activities of non-bank financial institutions in the United States pursuant to the Investment Advisers Act of

---

[9] Federal Reserve Board Supervisory Letter No. SR 96-10(SPE), Apr. 24, 1996.
[10] Federal Reserve Board Commercial Bank Examination Manual at 4128.1 (May 1998). See also Federal Reserve Board Bank Holding Company Supervision Manual at 2010.11.2.3 (Dec. 1998).

1940 (the Advisers Act). The Advisers Act imposes a fiduciary duty on U.S. investment advisers (whether registered or not), which includes an affirmative obligation to act solely in the client's best interests at all times and to make full and fair disclosure of all material facts (particularly where the adviser's interests may conflict with the client's).[11] A U.S. adviser's activities are measured against a higher standard of conduct than that used for commercial transactions, and the SEC has made clear that, among other things, an adviser has a duty to obtain best execution for clients' securities transactions where the adviser has discretionary authority, a duty to ensure that the adviser's investment advice is suitable to the client's objectives, needs, and circumstances, a duty to avoid effecting personal securities transactions inconsistent with client interests, and a duty of loyalty to clients.[12] These requirements, together with the general anti-fraud provisions of Section 206 of the Advisers Act, establish a framework designed to eliminate conflicts of interest for U.S. advisers and prevent an adviser from over-reaching or taking unfair advantage of a client's trust.

Adherence to fiduciary standards requires compliance with multiple federal, state and foreign laws. These fundamental and comprehensive requirements establish a framework designed to assure that the holdings by a Regulated Banking Group of equity securities of a public utility in a fiduciary capacity are not used in any way to impermissibly support exposures to a public utility as principal, and do not provide a basis to exercise impermissible control over a public utility issuer.

C. FERC Precedent Consistently and Appropriately Distinguishes Between Fiduciary Holdings and Holdings as Principal

In prior cases granting blanket authorizations under Section 203(a), the Commission has distinguished between the form of utilities holdings, granting the right to acquire in fiduciary capacity without limitation but

---

[11] See, e.g., SEC v. Capital Gains Research Bureau, Inc., 375 U.S. 180, 84 S. Ct. 275, 11 L. Ed. 2d. 237 (1963).
[12] In re Michael L. Smirlock, Investment Advisers Act Release No. 1393 (Nov. 29, 1993); In re John G. Kinnard and Co., SEC No-Action Letter, 1973 WL 11848, Fed. Sec. L. Rep. (CCH) 79,662 (Nov. 30, 1973); Advisers Act Release No. 203 (Aug. 11, 1966); Advisers Act Release No. 232, 1968 WL 4015 (Oct. 16, 1968).

imposing limits on acquisitions in a proprietary capacity.[13] These decisions recognize that securities held in a fiduciary capacity do not confer the ability to control management of the issuer and therefore do not raise Section 203 concerns. Most recently, in the context of Order No. 667, the PUHCA 2005 final rule, FERC reiterated that passive investments in a fiduciary capacity do not raise issues of control that are relevant to Section 203 review and approval. There, FERC excused from books and records requirements passive investors, in response to comments by Barclays and Morgan Stanley:

> We agree with the majority of commenters that the Commission should exempt passive investors from section 1264. Passive investors do not exercise control over jurisdictional companies, and thus the Commission does not need access to their books and records for purposes of ensuring just and reasonable rates. In response to the comments of Barclays and Morgan Stanley, we will also clarify here that the exemption for passive investors applies to the following entities: mutual funds; passive investments in collective investment vehicles whose assets are managed by banks, savings and loan associations and their operating subsidiaries, or broker/dealers; and persons that directly, or indirectly through their subsidiaries or affiliates, buy and sell the securities of public utilities in the ordinary course of business as a broker/dealer, underwriter or fiduciary, and not exercising operational control over the public utility.

Order No. 667, 70 Fed. Reg. at 75609 119. FERC referenced its own precedent—Shaw Plasma Power—establishing that passive investors are not electric utilities.[14] In view of the regulatory constraints to which they are subject and the obligation to the customers, FERC properly determined

---

[13] UBS AG and Bank of America, N.A., 101 FERC 61,312 (Dec. 19, 2002), reh 'g granted in part and denied in part, 103 FERC 61,284 (June 5, 2003), reh'g granted, 105 FERC 61,078 (Oct. 22, 2003); JPMorgan Chase Bank, N.A., Docket No. ER05-283 (letter order dated March 18, 2005).

[14] In DE Shaw Plasma Power LLC, 102 FERC 61,184 (2000), the passive investors simply held ownership interests in a company that indirectly held an interest in Plasma Power, did not own or operate jurisdictional facilities, and had no rights to direct, manage, or control the day-to-day operations of Plasma Portfolios or Plasma Power: "Apart from their equity investment and the holding of the Passive Veto Rights, the Passive Investors will not themselves have a voice or be involved in activities, jurisdictional or otherwise, that are to be conducted by Plasma Power."

that fiduciary holdings do not raise issues of control. The same determination should be made under newly-enacted Section 203(a)(2).

D. Request for Determination or Blanket Authorization for Fiduciary Investments by Non-Bank Affiliates of Banks

The acquisition of utility securities by the non-utility subsidiaries of Regulated Banking Groups in the ordinary course of business is exactly the kind of behavior that EPAct 2005 sought to encourage. Congressional intent was to streamline regulatory burdens to increase capital investment in the energy sector.[15] Applying Section 203 prior approval to fiduciary holdings would constrain the amount of capital that is allocated to the utility sector by financial enterprises—an adverse policy result.[16] For these reasons, and because no control issues are raised in view of the nature of fiduciary holdings of, and the protections provided by the regulatory schemes applicable to, Regulated Banking Groups, BofA and JPMCB seek a determination that fiduciary investments by their non-bank financial institutions are excluded from the scope of Section 203(a)(2) or in the alternative request blanket authorization for such fiduciary investments.

V. THE COMMISSION SHOULD CLARIFY THAT ITS PRIOR BLANKET AUTHORIZATIONS FOR BANKS' UNDERWRITING AND HEDGING ACTIVITIES APPLY TO SECTION 203(a)(2) AS WELL AS TO SECTION 203(a)(1).

FERC should clarify that the full extent of the relief that it has granted bank power marketers under market based rate orders issued under FPA Section 203(a)(1) also extends to holding companies under Section 203(a)(2). Under EPAct 2005, many banks which are public utilities will be newly classified

---

[15] S. Comm. on Energy & Natural Resources, Conference Report Summary by Title, at 12, (repealing PUHCA intended "to encourage investment in the nation's electricity infrastructure"); 151 Cong. Rec. S9256 (daily ed. July 28, 2005) (statement of Sen. Domenici that repealing PUHCA 1935 should bring additional investment).

[16] Far from expanding FERC jurisdiction over financial institutions, the definition of "holding company," set forth in section 1262(8)(B) of EPAct 2005, expressly excludes any company that owns, controls or holds with power to vote 10% or more of the outstanding voting securities of any public-utility company in its capacity as a bank or broker or dealer, subject to certain limitations.

as holding companies. Congress enacted a statutory exclusion for certain holdings of banks, bank operating subsidiaries, and broker-dealers from the definition of holding company in Section 1262(8) of EPAct 2005. Certainly the statutory exemption specifically covers loan collateral, loan liquidation and fiduciary holdings. BofA and JPMCB ask that FERC confirm the availability of blanket authorization under Section 203(a)(2) for failed underwritings and hedging holdings coextensive with the terms and conditions imposed in FERC market-based rate orders granting relief to bank power marketers under Section 203(a).

Absent the requested relief, the carefully crafted authorizations previously granted banks to enable them to continue their normal investment activities would become moot.

A. **Relationship Between the Relief that FERC Has Previously Granted to Banks under the Acquisition of Securities Clause and the New Statutory Exemption for Bank Fiduciary and Loan Holdings**

In recent years, a number of banks have become power marketers. Under the acquisitionof-securities clause of Section 203, electric utilities may not acquire securities of other electric utilities without FERC approval and "securities" is defined to include debt instruments.[17] If a bank becomes a power marketer (as opposed to establishing a power marketing affiliate), the bank becomes a public utility for purposes of FPA Section 203.

As discussed above, FERC has granted a number of special authorizations under Section 203(a) to bank power marketers in view of their need to continue participation in debt and equity investment activities, including authorizations in excess of the otherwise-applicable 5% limit for:

- Debt securities and dealer/trader activities.
- Fiduciary holdings.
- Acquisition of utility securities in connection with underwritings for 45 days; in the case of failed underwritings, the authorization is extended if the bank files within 45 days for Section 203 approval

---

[17] 18 C.F.R. § 34.1(b)(2).

to retain the securities and commits not to vote the securities held as a result of the failed underwriting.
- Holdings as principal for derivatives hedging purposes where bank regulators allow such holdings (under "safety and soundness" principles) provided that the bank commits not to vote more than 5%.[18]

In contrast, the statutory exemption under EPAct 2005, excluding banks and bank operating subsidiaries from the definition of "holding company" for purposes of Section 203(a)(2), applies to bank holdings that are:

- held as collateral for a loan;
- held in the ordinary course of business as a fiduciary; or
- acquired solely for purposes of liquidation and in connection with a loan previously contracted for and owned beneficially for a period of not more than 2 years.[19]

Under Order No. 669 as issued, as explained in more detail below, a bank parent power marketer to the extent that it directly or indirectly owns EWGs or QFs would qualify as a "holding company;" holding companies are required to seek pre-acquisition approval under Section 203(a)(2) unless an exclusion such as the bank/broker-dealer exemption or the 10% blanket authorization applies.

Thus, there is a disconnect between the broader scope of the blanket authorization in the power marketer approval order and the narrower statutory exclusion under Section 203(a)(2). Blanket approval for any level of voting equity holdings in EWGs or any other utilities applies under the power marketer approval order to loan related holdings, fiduciary holdings,

---

[18] JPMorgan Chase Bank, N.A., Docket No. ER05-283 (letter order dated Mar. 18, 2005); UBS AG and Bank of America N.A., 101 FERC 61,312 (2002), reh 'g granted in part and denied in part, 103 FERC 61,284 (2003), reh. granted, 105 FERC 61,078 (2003).

[19] EPAct 2005 § 1262(8)(B)(i). A broker-dealer is exempt if its holdings are (i) not beneficially owned by the broker or dealer and are subject to any voting instructions which may be given by the customers or their assigns or (ii) acquired within 12 months in the ordinary course of business as a broker, dealer or underwriter with the bona fide intention of effecting distribution of the specific securities so acquired. Id. § 1262(8)(B)(ii).

underwriting holdings limited to 45 days, and hedging derivative transactions. Since the statutory exclusion under Section 203(a)(2) covers only the first two categories—loan related holdings and fiduciary holdings—BofA and JPMCB request confirmation that bank parent power marketers which have obtained FERC relief under Section 203(a)(1) similarly enjoy a blanket authorizations from any potentially applicable pre-acquisition requirements that could arise under Section 203(a)(2) if the banks are classified as holding companies by virtue, for example, of EWG or QF ownership. The same policy reasons that led FERC to grant waiver from the Section 203(a)(1) requirements would apply to banks classified as holding companies under Section 203(a)(2), viz., the desire to have well-capitalized institutions participate in the energy sector, acknowledgment of the need to provide relief from the acquisition of securities clause to reflect that banks hold utility securities in the ordinary course of their core business, and extensive oversight by federal bank regulators.

1.   Extension of the 45 Day Holding Period for Failed Underwritings

FERC carefully assessed the need for banks to benefit from authorization of underwriting-related holdings in the UBS/Bank of America proceedings and subsequently granted the same relief to JPMorgan and other bank power marketers. Under Paragraph 13 of the June 5, 2003 Bank of America/UBS Order, voting equity securities of public utilities acquired in connection with underwriting activities initially were to be subject to the 5% limitation if they are not disposed of or sold within 45 days of the underwriting. UBS and Bank of America requested and received modification of this condition because it would have been unworkable from a practical standpoint and would have created a significant risk of inadvertent noncompliance with Section 203.

In a successful underwriting, the underwriter purchases shares from the issuer and immediately resells those shares in the market. In a failed underwriting, the underwriter is not able to resell those shares immediately and will attempt to sell the unsold shares in an orderly manner over a period of time following the closing of the initial purchase.

When banks act as underwriters, they will not know at the outset whether they will be successful in disposing of a sufficient number of shares to assure that their holdings do not exceed 5% of the issuer after 45 days. In attempting to assure compliance with the approval requirements of Section 203, however, they would be obligated to seek the Commission's approval immediately to retain the shares or risk noncompliance; even then, there can be no assurance that approval would be timely granted.

The need to make a public application to the Commission for this purpose could send a negative signal to the market and could significantly affect the price at which the shares could be sold, injuring not just the underwriter, but the public utility issuer as well. In addition, if the banks did do not receive the Commission's approval within the 45 days, they would have to sell the shares under fire sale conditions to the disadvantage of the issuer.

Accordingly, after detailed consideration, FERC granted Bank of America/UBS relief in its second order on rehearing.[20] FERC noted that the bank applicants had proposed as conditions that the Commission provide that the exemption for securities acquired in an underwriting capacity will end after the expiration of the 45-day period unless the underwriter (i) has within that period filed an application under Section 203 to retain the securities, and (ii) has undertaken during the pendency of such application not to vote the securities held. This modification alleviated any concern the Commission may have that the underwriting exemption could be used to avoid the 5% limitation on holding equity securities as principal. It would also prevent the underwriter from exercising any voting control over a public utility while attempting an orderly disposition of shares acquired in an underwriting capacity. In addition, by allowing the underwriter to file an application by the end of the 45-day period, the Commission would substantially lessen the possibility that the filing of a disclosure notice of the holdings could adversely affect the market for the issuer's shares. More generally, FERC noted that "such acquisitions would not ordinarily allow Petitioners to control other public utilities," that "[t]he Federal Reserve has found that underwriting activities by banks are consistent with the provisions of the BHC Act relevant to ownership or

---

[20] UBS AG and Bank of America N.A., reh 'g granted in part and denied in part, 103 FERC 61,284 (June 5, 2003).

APPENDICES

control of non-banking entities," and that "Congress has deemed it unnecessary to subject underwriting activities to pre-approval by antitrust authorities."[21]

Finally, we note that in the broker-dealer exclusion in Section 1262(8)(B)(ii) of EPAct 2005, Congress authorized underwriting holdings provided that there is a bona fide intention of effecting distribution within 12 months.

2. Treatment of Securities Acquired for Derivative/Hedging Purposes

A bank engages in hedging transactions which are intended to reduce the risk to the bank of engaging in its permissible derivative business. As the Office of the Comptroller of the Currency (OCC) concluded in its Interpretive Letter No. 892 (Sept. 13, 2000):

National banks may engage in customer-driven equity derivative transactions as part of the business of banking. Hedging risks arising from these permissible banking activities is an essential and integral part of those banking activities. The [Bank's] use of equities to hedge permissible equity derivative transactions provides the most accurate, least costly hedges, and thus is convenient and useful in conducting permissible banking activities, and incidental to the business of banking.

Paragraph 14 of the June 5, 2003 UBS/Bank of America Order initially would have counted within the 5% limitation acquisitions of public utility securities in connection with applicants' derivative/hedging activities.[22] FERC noted that the bank regulators "allow banks to acquire equity securities, subject to a limitation of 5% of the stock of any issuer, solely for the purpose of hedging the bank's exposure arising from customer-driven equity derivative transactions." Subsequently, Bank of America and UBS sought and obtained relief from the otherwise applicable 5% limitation on hedging activities under certain circumstances.

---

[21] 103 FERC 61,284 at 13.
[22] 103 FERC 61,284 at 14.

165

The OCC, the primary federal regulator of national banks (like Bank of America and JPMorgan Chase Bank), considers the 5% limitation on securities held for hedging purposes to be a supervisory standard which may be exceeded in appropriate circumstances with OCC concurrence. Thus, for example, the OCC might consider it prudent to allow an equity derivative hedge to exceed 5% where stock price movements indicate that, to protect the safety and soundness of the bank, the bank should hedge its exposure on underlying derivative transactions with the acquisition of additional shares. There may also be situations where the actions of the issuer to redeem or otherwise reduce its outstanding equity securities result in a bank's pre-existing hedge exceeding 5% of the security class at issue (but where the regulator concurs that the greater-than-5% position fulfills an appropriate risk-reduction function). Moreover, there is, as a practical matter, no prospect that bank regulators would permit a bank to deviate from the 5% supervisory standard if the purpose of doing so would be to permit the bank to acquire or exercise control over the issuer.

B.   Clarification Requested that Relief Granted under Former Section 203(a) (now Section 203(a)(1)) Will Continue to Apply to Banks under Section 203(a)(2)

For these reasons, FERC's October 22, 2003 Order subsequently granted UBS/Bank of America the relief requested, recognizing that the application of the 5% limitation to banks' holdings of equity securities for hedging purposes would be inconsistent, and possibly at cross-purposes, with the bank regulatory regime.[23] The Banks' commitment to not vote derivative and failed underwriting holdings in excess of 5% was recognized by FERC as yet another safeguard. Similar approval has been included in similar orders issued to JPMorgan and other bank power marketers.

There is a need for the Commission to harmonize the exclusions under Section 203(a)(2) to meet those previously granted by FERC after careful consideration Section 203(a)(1). BofA and JPMCB respectfully request, therefore, that Order No. 669 be clarified to authorize (i) underwriting holdings to exceed 45 days, and (ii) equity derivative hedging holdings, to

---

[23] UBS AG and Bank of America N.A., order on reh 'g, 105 FERC 61,078 (Oct. 22, 2003) § C.

the extent permitted under FERC's prior orders applicable to bank power marketers.

VI. BANKS AND THEIR SIBLING ENTITIES THAT ARE EXCLUSIVELY "HOLDING COMPANIES" BY VIRTUE OF QF AND EWG INTERESTS SHOULD BE RELIEVED FROM SECTION 203 APPROVAL REQUIREMENTS

As several financial institutions have already advised the Commission,[24] application of Section 203(a)(2) pre-acquisition approval requirements to holding companies by virtue of their interests in EWGs and QFs would impose serious unintended consequences on financial institutions that routinely acquire debt and equity securities. BofA and JPMCB will demonstrate below that the result is: (i) inconsistent with the intent of EPAct 2005 (which was to repeal onerous holding company regulation); (ii) inconsistent with the statutory exemption for specific bank and broker-dealer holdings; and (iii) unnecessary as a screen to filter out acquisitions that may exacerbate market power.

A. The Genesis of the Problem

As enacted by Section 1289 of EPAct 2005, Section 203(a)(2) imposes pre-acquisition pre-approval requirements on entities that are "holding companies" in a "holding company system that includes a transmitting utility or an electric utility." By drafting oversight, the definition of "holding company" in Section 203(a)(6), which cross-references EPAct 2005 § 1262(8), includes companies that own 10% or more of the outstanding voting securities EWGs and QFs.

As FERC is well aware, all qualifying cogeneration facilities and certain small power production facilities were exempt from status as an "electric utility company" under Section 210(f) of PUHCA 1935 and FERC's implementing rules. 18 C.F.R. § 292.601. EWGs were exempted by Section 32(e) from classification as an "electric utility company" or a "public-utility company" under PUHCA 1935. As a consequence, a company that owned

---

[24] E.g., Comments of GE Energy Financial Services; Morgan Stanley Capital Group; and Goldman Sachs, Docket RM05-34-000.

or controlled 10% or more of the outstanding voting securities of a QF or EWG did not, by virtue of such ownership, become a "holding company" under PUHCA 1935.

All companies classified as holding companies, even if they are only holding companies by virtue of QF and EWG ownership, must seek pre-acquisition approval of the acquisition of any security with a value in excess of $10 million of (1) a "transmitting utility," (2) an "electric utility company," or (3) a holding company in a holding company system that includes (i) a transmitting utility or (ii) an electric utility company. FERC pre-approval is thereby required of any acquisition of any equity or debt with a value in excess of $10 million of any publicly-traded electric utility company or gas utility company, QF, EWG, or of a parent company of any QF or EWG. BofA and JPMCB recognize that Order No. 669 granted blanket authorization for acquisition of nonvoting securities and up to 10% of voting equity of utilities. However, contrary to the assertion in Order No. 669, this does not fully address the issue as holdings of EWGs and QFs may exceed 10%, and moreover it does not countenance deviation from the express Congressional intent to exclude EWGs and QFs from Section 203 as revised.

B.   Congress Did Not Intend That FERC Require Pre-Approval of Transactions by QF/EWG-Only Holding Companies

There is no indication that Congress intended to apply Section 203(a)(2) to QFs and EWGs. Under the status quo ante, FERC addressed under Section 203(a)(1): (i) acquisitions by another public utility of securities of a second public utility, and (ii) acquisitions by an entity that was not a FERC-jurisdictional "public utility" of voting securities only if the acquisition would result in a change in control over a public utility. While it is clear that Congress intended, in revising Section 203, in light of the repeal of PUHCA 1935, to give the Commission jurisdiction over acquisitions of traditional utilities by holding companies with traditional utility subsidiaries, there is no indication that Congress intended to require Commission approval for transactions that previously were not subject to PUHCA 1935 or FPA jurisdiction. Nothing in EPAct 2005 reflects a Congressional intent to expand the scope of the holding company definition. As Congressman Barton has cautioned, FERC should avoid an overly expansive, aggressive reading of its EPAct 2005 jurisdiction.[25] Accordingly, BofA and JPMCB believe that FERC's imposition of new burdens on owners of QFs and EWGs not associated with transmission-owning utilities misinterprets Congressional intent in EPAct 2005.

1. There Is No Indication that Congress Intended to Subject QFs to a Pre-Approval Requirement

As to QFs, QFs are not treated as electric utility companies under PUHCA 1935 nor are QFs electric utilities under pre-existing FERC FPA regulations. Under 18 CFR § 292.601(c), QFs are currently exempt from the requirement that an acquiror seek prior FERC approval under FPA Section 203. Order No. 669 would for the first time require FERC approval of acquisitions or mergers involving QFs or their owners.

FERC's rules may discourage investment in QFs, contrary to the evident intent of EPAct 2005, which revised the requirements of the Public Utility Regulatory Policies Act of 1978 (PURPA) in certain specific aspects but notably did not repeal PURPA. In fact, Sections 125 1-54 of EPAct 2005 continue in place FERC's statutory objective of continuing cogeneration.

Requiring FERC approval of acquisitions or mergers involving QFs or their owners would be at odds with the evident purpose of the EPAct amendments to FERC's Section 203 authority. Congress intended to transfer to FERC authority over holding company acquisitions that the SEC had exercised under PUHCA 1935. But the SEC never exercised authority over QF acquisitions and QFs were excluded from the definition of electric utility company under PUHCA 1935 such that their upstream owners were not holding companies.

---

[25] Comments of Rep. Joe Barton, Docket No. RM05-34 (Nov. 7, 2005) at 1 ("section 1289, like the PUHCA repeal subtitle, was not intended to expand significantly the Commission's jurisdiction or to provide for more burdensome regulations. The intent was to provide for regulatory streamlining and increased investment in the electric utility sector.")

2. **There Is No Indication that Congress Intended to Impose a Burden on EWG Ownership under EPACT 2005 that Did Not Exist under PUHCA 1935**

As to EWGs, FERC justifies its approach by pointing out that EWGs (unlike QFs) are electric utilities under FPA regulation. However, PUHCA 1935 excluded EWGs from the definition of electric utility company and their owners from holding company status. FERC says that its hands are tied because Congress enacted a definition of "holding company" in EPAct 2005 that encompasses EWGs. However, Congress certainly did not forget about the special treatment to be accorded EWGs. Section 1262(6) of EPAct 2005 incorporates a definition of EWG that states that the definition has the same meaning as under PUHCA 1935.[26]

C. Form of Relief

BofA and JPMCB can appreciate that FERC could determine that it is relevant to assessing the market power of a traditional utility holding company (e.g., one that owns transmission wires, or serves captive customers) to ascertain the extent of its generation market power. To achieve such an objective, however, it is not necessary to treat QFs as electric utility companies or to impose new regulatory approval costs on QFs, EWGs, and their owners.

Financial institutions regularly engage in the acquisition of debt and equity securities in QFs and EWGs. Banks and other financial institutions routinely acquire and sell debt and equity security interests with short transactional lead times. The need to obtain Commission approval for each such transaction and for other investments by virtue of the holding company status due to their ownership of QFs and EWGs would, due to inherent delay, impose a major impediment to financial transactions.

---

[26] "Exempt wholesale generator and foreign utility company. The terms "exempt wholesale generator" and "foreign utility company" have the same meanings as in sections 32 and 33, respectively, of the Public Utility Holding Company Act of 1935 (15 U.S.C. 79z-5a, 79z-5b), as those sections existed on the day before the effective date of this subtitle." (Emphasis added.)

To remedy this situation, it is not necessary that FERC change its conclusion that owners of QFs and EWGs qualify as holding companies. Alternatively, all that is necessary is to provide blanket authorization from Section 203 subject to appropriate conditions and safeguards, such as a status report to the Commission within 30 days following the acquisition, where companies are only holding companies by virtue of QF or EWG status. By analogy, FERC's PUHCA final rule appropriately established an exemption from books and records requirements to customer generation (automatically below 100 MW). So too a blanket authorization from Section 203 could apply where a company is only a holding company by virtue of EWG or QF ownership.

At a minimum, existing holdings in EWGs and QFs should be grandfathered. This would enable banks and their affiliates to adjust their future practices respecting EWGs and QFs to avoid such acquisitions from impacting the core aspects of their business.

VII. CONCLUSION

For the foregoing reasons, BofA and JPMCB respectfully request that the Commission grant hearing and/or clarification on the issues set forth above.

VIII. NOTICES AND COMMUNICATIONS

Notices and communications with regard to these proceedings should be addressed to:

Margaret M. Grieve
Bank of America
9 West 57th Street
New York, NY 10019
Phone: 646-313-8144
Email: margaret.grieves@bofasecurities.com

Ike I. Gibbs
JPMorgan Chase Bank, N.A. 270 Park Avenue, Floor 40
New York, NY 10017

Phone: 212-270-5877
Email: ike.i.gibbs@jpmchase.com

Sara D. Schotland, Esq.
Cleary Gottlieb Steen & Hamilton LLP
2000 Pennsylvania Avenue, N.W., Suite 9000 Washington, D.C. 20006
Phone: (202) 974-1500
Email: sschotland@cgsh.com
Counsel for Bank of America, N.A. and JPMorgan Chase Bank, N.A.

    Respectfully submitted,

    /s/ Sara D. Schotland
    Sara D. Schotland
    CLEARY GOTTLIEB STEEN & HAMILTON LLP
    2000 Pennsylvania Avenue, N.W., Suite 9000
    Washington, D.C. 20006
    Telephone: (202) 974-1500
    Dated: January 23, 2006

CERTIFICATE OF SERVICE

I hereby certify that copies of the foregoing Request for Clarification and/or Rehearing were served upon each person designated on the official service list compiled by the Secretary in this proceeding via electronic mail, where available, otherwise by U.S. mail, postage prepaid.

Dated at Washington, D.C. this 23rd day of January 2006.

/s/ Jennifer A. Morrissey
CLEARY GOTTLIEB STEEN & HAMILTON LLP
2000 Pennsylvania Avenue, N.W., Suite 9000
Washington, D.C. 20006
Telephone: (202) 974-1500

Courtesy of Sara Schotland, Cleary, Gottlieb, Steen & Hamilton

APPENDIX B

PRO-COMPANY LICENSE WITH A UNIVERSITY

License Agreement

This Agreement is made and entered into as of _____, 200__ (the "Effective Date"), by and between [_____ University] ("University"), a _____, and [Client Company] Inc. ("Licensee"), a _____ corporation. University and Licensee are sometimes referred to as a "Party" or as the "Parties."

WHEREAS, University is owner by assignment from the following inventors, _____ and _____, of their entire right, title and interest in certain patent applications and patent rights as more fully described in Appendix ___ to this Agreement;

WHEREAS, Licensee wishes to obtain the exclusive worldwide license in order to practice in the field defined herein the above referenced inventions covered by patent rights in the United States and in foreign countries, and to manufacture, use and sell in the commercial market the products made in accordance therewith; and

WHEREAS, in accordance with its policy to seek use and application of University inventions for the benefit of the public, University wishes to grant such a license to Licensee in accordance with the terms of this Agreement.

NOW THEREFORE, in consideration of the foregoing premises and their mutual covenants contained herein, the Parties hereby agree as follows:

ARTICLE I - DEFINITIONS

1.1   "Affiliates" shall mean any company, corporation, or business that directly or indirectly owns or controls at least fifty percent (50%) of the voting stock of Licensee, or in which Licensee or Licensee's Affiliate directly or indirectly owns or controls at least fifty percent (50%) of the voting stock or other voting equity interests.

1.2   "Bona Fide Proposal" means a proposal submitted by a third party to University in which the third party proposes in good faith to license any of the Patent Rights in any Subfield for which the Licensee has not met the Diligence Criteria as described in Paragraph 2.4(f), where such third party demonstrates to University and Licensee that it has access to funding and resources sufficient to introduce products utilizing Patent Rights into the commercial market.

1.3   "Bulk Net Sales" shall mean the Net Sales realized by Licensee or its Affiliates or Sublicensees from sale(s) of Licensed Products to Distributors. Where a particular unit of Licensed Product has been sold to a Distributor in a transaction that generates Bulk Net Sales hereunder, no further sales or distribution of that Licensed Product unit will be part of the Net Sales hereunder.

1.4   "Diligence Criteria" means the level of effort to be required from Licensee and/or Affiliates or Sublicensees or Distributors with respect to each of the Subfields in order to avoid the application, following the _____ anniversary of the Effective Date, of University's rights under Paragraph 2.4(f) with respect to such Subfield. At any given time (the "Applicable Time"), the Diligence Criteria for a Subfield shall be satisfied if any of Licensee or its Affiliates or its or their Sublicensees or Distributors meet the criteria stated in either or both of the following two clauses:

  (i)   it or they have, prior to the expiration of _____ months following the Effective Date, [DESCRIBE CRITERION]; provided, however, that if Licensee and its Affiliates, Sublicensees, and Distributors are or have been prevented in whole or in part from satisfying such criterion by actions or failures of University, or by factors or considerations that similarly prevent others generally from doing so, then such _____-month period will be tolled during the period in which such actions, failures, factors, or considerations have such effect;

  (ii) it or they are conducting or sponsoring activities intended to discover, formulate, develop, test, manufacture, license, protect, or certify any one or more Licensed Products within such Subfield, where the aggregate sums expended or budgeted (or, as to subsequent fiscal years, demonstrably anticipated to be expended or budgeted) by Licensee and its Affiliates and its or their Sublicensees or Distributors in support thereof are either (x) at least $_____$ for Licensee's current fiscal year that includes the Applicable Time (whether such year started before or after the ____ anniversary of the Effective Date), or (y) at least $_____$ for such current fiscal year and at least $_____$ in the aggregate for such current fiscal year and for either the immediately preceding fiscal year or the immediately following fiscal year, it being agreed that such sums may include, without limitation, any or all of the following sorts of expenditures or budgeted expenditures:

(A) research related expenditures or budgeted expenditures;

(B) expenditures or budgeted expenditures related to _____ or preparing for the same or evaluating or reporting on the results of the same;

(C) expenditures or budgeted expenditures for the preparation of, documentation of, application for, or maintenance of patents that bear directly upon such Subfield; and

(D) an allocated portion of Licensee's and its Affiliates' and its or their Sublicensees' or Distributors' fully burdened costs of labor, benefits, systems support, supplies, equipment, facilities, travel, outside services, and general and administrative functions, all as attributable to work done or budgeted to be done with respect to such Licensed Products within such Subfield;

it being agreed that, where particular activities are directed at a Subfield and also at another Subfield or Subfields due to the overlap of such Subfields, the expenditures and budgeted expenditures involved shall for purposes of this clause (ii) be attributed in full to each of such Subfields.

1.5 "<u>Distributor</u>" shall mean a non-Affiliate third party to which Licensed Products are sold for redistribution, with or without further processing, formulation or repackaging, and that are not acquired by such third party as an End User or made by or for it as a Sublicensee. Where the same party is both a Distributor and a Sublicensee with respect to different units of Licensed Products, sales to it and by it will be treated separately for purposes of this Agreement. For example, those Licensed Products sold to it in its role as a Distributor will be covered by Section 3.4, and those Licensed Products sold to it or by it in its role as a Sublicensee shall be covered by Section 3.3.

1.6 "End User" shall mean a person that acquires Licensed Products for end-use or for retail sale, and not for redistribution to any third party that is not an End User.

1.7 "End User Net Sales" shall mean the Net Sales realized by Licensee or its Affiliates or Sublicensees from commercial sales of Licensed Products to End Users, together with the right for such End Users to practice the applicable End-Use Processes, if any, in connection with such Licensed Products.

1.8 "Excluded Revenues" shall mean any and all payments and other consideration, whether in cash or in-kind, received or receivable by Licensee or its Affiliates (or, with respect to Subclause 2.4(f)(ii)(C), by University) to the extent attributable to equity investments; loans; research or development support; equipment or facilities acquisitions; patent and other supplier or advisor costs and reimbursements; the sale or lease of any materials other than Licensed Products; or any other goods or services provided or rendered or to be provided or rendered, including in each case fees, expenses, overhead and profit.

1.9 "Fee Revenues" shall mean, other than Excluded Revenues, any up-front license fees, option or option exercise fees, contingent milestone payments, and other fees (other than sales-based royalties) realized by Licensee or its Affiliates (or, with respect to Subclause 2.4(f)(ii)(C), by University) as consideration for the grant of any sublicense of Patent Rights to a Sublicensee, or as consideration for entering into a supply agreement with a Distributor (other than as the price of Licensed Products sold to the Distributor), or any other similar transaction that exploits the use of Patent Rights (e.g., option agreement) to the extent attributable to the Patent

Rights and the Licensed Products (or, with respect to Subclause 2.4(f)(ii)(C), any transaction by University there described). Where any Patent Rights are sublicensed, or a supply agreement or any other similar transaction is entered, in conjunction with the grant of other rights or interests of any kind or with entering into a supply or other agreement with respect to any products or services other than Licensed Products, the aggregate of any fees or other such consideration not associated with the sublicense of Patent Rights or with the agreement to supply Licensed Products or other similar transaction that exploits the use of Patent Rights shall for purposes hereof be allocated by Licensee in a manner that consistently and equitably reflects the contribution of the sublicense to the Patent Rights, the agreement to supply Licensed Products, and/or any other similar agreement.

1.10 "Field" shall mean _____, together with research and development activities directed toward _____.

1.11 "Licensed Processes" shall mean processes the making, using, or selling of which, when and where occurring, would, but for a license granted under this Agreement, constitute infringement of any issued and valid claims in the Patent Rights.

1.12 "Licensed Products" shall mean products (i) the making, using, or selling of which, when and where occurring, would, but for a license granted under this Agreement, constitute infringement of any issued and valid claims in the Patent Rights or (ii) that are specially designed or formulated for use or application in Licensed Processes.

1.13 "Net Sales" shall mean the gross amount realized by Licensee or its Affiliates or Sublicensees from sales of Licensed Products less: (a) customary trade, quantity or cash discounts and non-affiliated brokers' or agents' commissions actually allowed and taken; (b) government mandated rebates and retroactive price reductions; (c) shipping and insurance costs; (d) Amounts repaid or credited by reason of rejection, recall or return; and/or (e) taxes, duties, and surcharges levied on and/or other governmental charges made as to production, sale, transportation, exportation, importation, delivery, or use. Net Sales shall be calculated in accordance with US generally accepted accounting principles consistently applied. Net Sales will not include any sales, sublicenses, transfers or other distributions or dispositions made at no charge, or for testing, developmental or regulatory purposes, or in connection with charitable purposes or for promotional purposes. Sale of any Licensed Product between Licensee, its Affiliates or their Sublicensees and another entity in such group (other than where the buyer is an End User), shall not be counted as part of Net Sales. In such cases, "Net Sales" hereunder shall be determined using the gross amount realized by the transferee after sale to Distributors or End Users, less the qualifying costs allowed under this section and applicable only to the sale to the Distributor or End User.

Where a Licensed Product is sold in the form of a combination product containing one or more [patented] components which are themselves not Licensed Products and such Licensed Product and such other components are also sold separately during the applicable royalty reporting period in the country in which the sale of the combination product was made, the Net Sales shall be calculated by multiplying the sales price of such combination product by the fraction $A/(A+B)$ where A is the invoice price of such Licensed Product when sold separately and B is the total invoice price of such other components when sold separately. If separate sales of both such Licensed Product and such other components did not occur in such period, then the respective invoice prices in the most recent royalty reporting period in which sales of both occurred in such country will be used, provided that such prior period did not end more than one year before the end of the period in which such combination product is sold. Where such Licensed Product is sold separately during such periods but the other components are not, Net Sales for the combination product shall be determined by multiplying actual Net Sales of the combination product (as if the entire combination product were such a Licensed Product) during the royalty reporting period by the ratio of the average per-unit sale price of such Licensed Product when sold separately to the average per-unit Net Sales of the combination product, in each case during the applicable royalty reporting period in the country in which the sale of the combination product was made. Where such other components are sold separately during such periods but such Licensed Product is not, Net Sales for the combination product shall be determined by multiplying actual Net Sales of the combination product (as if the entire combination product were such a Licensed Product) during the royalty reporting period by the difference obtained by subtracting from 1 the ratio of the average per-unit sale price of such other components when sold separately to the average per-unit Net Sales of the combination product, in each case during the applicable royalty reporting period in the country in which the sale of the combination product was made. If such average sales price cannot be determined for either of such Licensed Product or for such other components included in the combination product, Net Sales for purposes of determining payments under this Agreement shall be calculated by multiplying the Net Sales of the combination product (as if the entire combination product were such a Licensed Product) by the fraction C/C+D where C is the standard, fully absorbed cost of such Licensed Product's portion of the combination and D is the sum of the standard, fully absorbed costs of such other components included in the combination product, in each case as determined in accordance with US generally accepted accounting principles consistently applied; provided, however that the Parties then agree that such approach is valid in light of the particular circumstances, which agreement shall not be unreasonably withheld or delayed.

1.14   "Patent Rights" means the U.S. and international patent applications listed in Appendix ___ to this Agreement and any divisions, continuations, and continuations-in-part to the extent the claims are directed to the subject matter and claim priority to such applications; patents issuing thereon or reissues thereof; and any and all corresponding U.S. and foreign patents and patent applications, which will be automatically incorporated in and added to this Agreement and shall periodically be added to Appendix ___ attached to this Agreement and made part thereof.

1.15   "Subfield(s)" shall mean each of the Subfield(s) [defined as follows: _____] [listed in Appendix ___].

1.16   "Sublicensee" shall mean a non-Affiliate third party to which Licensee, or another Sublicensee, grants an express sublicense under the Patent Rights to make, use or sell the Licensed Products or to practice the Licensed Processes, it being understood that for purposes hereof, a third party that acquires a Licensed Product shall, without becoming a Sublicensee hereunder, thereby obtain the right to use, sell and import that Licensed Product and to practice the Licensed Processes in connection with such use, sale or import.

ARTICLE II - GRANT

2.1 University hereby grants to Licensee and Affiliates and Licensee accepts, subject to the terms and conditions hereof, the worldwide exclusive license under the Patent Rights to make, use, sell, offer for sale, and import Licensed Products, and to practice the Licensed Processes, in the Field. Such license shall include the right to grant sublicenses in accordance with Section 2.2. University agrees it will not grant licenses under Patent Rights to others in the Field except as required by University's obligations in Paragraph 2.4(a), and except as provided in Paragraph 2.4(f).

2.2 Licensee shall have the same responsibility for the activities of any Sublicensee as if the activities were directly those of Licensee. Licensee shall provide University with the name, contact information and address of any Sublicensee and with a copy of any sublicense agreements that would grant the Sublicensee an exclusive sublicense under the Licensed Patents in any field of use in the Field, such copy to be provided at least thirty (30) days prior to execution by Licensee of such sublicense agreement. Licensee shall give careful consideration to any reasonable objections presented by University with respect to such exclusive sublicense, to the extent University's interests are directly implicated. Licensee agrees that sublicenses granted hereunder shall provide that they will not be transferable by the Sublicensee to a third party unless such transfer is made by the Sublicensee to any purchaser of all or substantially all of the assets to which such sublicense agreement shall be binding upon and inure to the benefit of said purchaser or successor in interest. Licensee shall notify University of the name and contact information of the transferee within 30 days of the occurrence of such transfer.

2.3 The term of this Agreement and the exclusive license set forth in Section 2.1 (the "License Term") shall be from the Effective Date until the expiration of the last to expire of the Patent Rights.

2.4 The granting and acceptance of this license is subject to the following conditions:

(a) Any right granted in this Agreement greater than that permitted under Public Law 96-517 or Public Law 98-620 shall be subject to modification as may be required to conform to the provision of that statute.

(b) Licensee agrees that Licensed Products sold in the United States by it, its Affiliates or its Sublicensees, if and to the extent the same make use of any government-supported aspect of the Patent Rights, will be manufactured substantially in the United States, unless a waiver of this requirement is duly obtained from the appropriate federal agency. University will upon request promptly and diligently seek to obtain, or assist Licensee to obtain, any such waiver(s) in appropriate circumstances.

(c) University reserves the right for itself to use the subject matter described and claimed in Patent Rights for non-commercial research purposes. Provided that Licensee has maintained its rights under this Agreement and except as provided in Paragraph 2.4(f), no such subject matter may be commercialized in any way, whether by University or by any sponsor, contractor or other licensee of either of them, without the prior agreement of Licensee, which agreement University acknowledges has not been granted and may be withheld in Licensee's discretion. The University agrees that during the term of the License Agreement, it will not enter into a research agreement sponsored by a for-profit entity involving any of the inventors named in the Recitals to this Agreement if such research would require use of the Patent Rights, without first obtaining the consent of Licensee, which consent shall not be unreasonably withheld so long as Licensee's rights hereunder are preserved and reasonable mechanisms are put in place to avoid confusion as to the Parties' rights and interests. Mindful of the University's prerogatives to conduct research using public funds, the Parties acknowledge that such inventors may participate in research projects funded solely by public or philanthropic agencies that would require research use of Patent Rights, so long as the rights granted to such agencies do not diminish the rights granted to Licensee herein.

(d) Licensee shall pay or cause to be paid any future costs connected with its or its Affiliates' or Sublicensees' commercial development of the Licensed Products, including but not limited to the costs of complying with applicable governmental testing, approvals and regulations.

(e) Licensee shall use commercially reasonable efforts to effect introduction of the Licensed Products into the commercial market as soon as practicable, consistent with sound and reasonable business practices and judgment in the prevailing regulatory environment, it being understood, however, that the Licensee does not commit that any Licensed Products will be successfully developed or marketed, or, if marketed, that any particular level of royalties will be available therefrom to University. After first market introduction of Licensed Product(s) hereunder, and until the expiration of this Agreement, Licensee shall endeavor to keep one or more Licensed Products reasonably available to the public. University's rights under Paragraph 2.4(f) shall be its sole remedies for any failure or failures of Licensee to comply with this or any other diligence condition or obligation.

(f) In order to preserve opportunity for maximal public use of Patent Rights, if, at any Applicable Time after _____ (_) years from the Effective Date, the Diligence Criteria for any particular Subfield are not then satisfied, then:

(i) the University shall have the right to market Patent Rights and seek companies interested in licensing Patent Rights in that Subfield, provided that University shall first notify Licensee of the Subfield involved and of University's intention to do so at least 90 days prior to undertaking any activities to do so, unless Licensee satisfies the Diligence Criteria as to such Subfield within 90 days following the date of such notice, in which case this clause (i) shall not apply unless and until another Applicable Time at which the Diligence Criteria for such Subfield are not then satisfied; and

(ii) if University thereafter receives a Bona Fide Proposal from a third party with respect to any project or product within that Subfield, University shall so notify Licensee, and University shall have the right to compel Licensee to do one of the following, at the choice of the Licensee:

(A) unless University has given Licensee the notice provided for in clause (i) above within the immediately preceding 12 months and Licensee did not satisfy the Diligence Criteria for the applicable Subfield within the 90-day period there described (in which event Licensee need not be given another opportunity to do so under this subclause (ii)(A)), if Licensee satisfies the Diligence Criteria for the applicable Subfield within 90 days following such notice under this clause (ii), then this clause (ii) shall not apply unless and until another Applicable Time at which the Diligence Criteria for such Subfield are not then satisfied;

(B) Licensee may sublicense Patent Rights in such Subfield to the third party that submitted the Bona Fide Proposal, on terms and conditions consistent with this Agreement and otherwise as may be determined by Licensee and such third party, provided that Licensee remains reasonably diligent in attempting to secure agreement upon such a sublicense; or

(C) Licensee shall, if neither subclause (A) nor subclause (B) above are applicable, cause licensed Patent Rights to revert to University in such Subfield so that University may license Patent Rights to the third party that made the Bona Fide Proposal, in each case with a scope and in substance sufficient for the conduct by University and such third party of the program or project in such Subfield contemplated under such Bona Fide Proposal, it being understood that University shall use good faith efforts to negotiate a sharing of patent costs of the sort referred to in Article VI below incurred following the date hereof that reasonably reflects the scope of such third party agreement. If such license is so granted, University shall pay Licensee a running fee equal to _____ percent (____%) of all sales-based royalties and all Fee Revenues received by University or University or their Affiliates or assigns under or in connection with such license to such third party.

In no event shall Licensee be required to make any grant, whether express or by implication, under a third-party sublicense or otherwise, of any right to use, access, practice, or otherwise exploit any know-how, data, materials, technology, or patent rights of, or that may be available to, Licensee or its Affiliates that are not part of the Patent Rights.

(g) All sublicenses granted by Licensee hereunder shall include a requirement consistent with Paragraph 2.4(e) that the Sublicensee use its commercially reasonable efforts to bring the subject matter of the sublicenses into commercial use as quickly as is reasonably possible. Licensee or its Affiliate shall bind the Sublicensee to meet Licensee's obligations to University under this Agreement, and shall attach a copy of this Agreement to such sublicense agreements. Copies of all agreements that grant sublicenses hereunder to Sublicensees or that constitute supply agreements with Distributors with respect to Licensed Products, or any other similar transaction that exploits the use of Patent Rights shall be provided to University.

(h) A license in any other field of use in addition to the Field shall be the subject of a separate agreement and shall require Licensee's submission of evidence, satisfactory to University, demonstrating its willingness and ability to develop and commercialize the kinds of products or processes likely to be encompassed in such other field. If University has non-exclusively licensed in such other field prior to Licensee's request, and the University has determined to grant Licensee rights in the additional Field, University shall grant to Licensee a non-exclusive license under terms and conditions at least as favorable as the previous non-exclusive license.

2.5   All rights reserved to the United States Government and others under Public Law 96-517 and 98-620 shall remain and shall in no way be affected by this Agreement. To the extent that any invention under the

Patent Rights constitutes a subject invention under any grant or support from the U.S. government, University represents and warrants that it has duly and timely filed with the proper government officials all invention disclosures with respect to such Patent Rights, as required by such grant or other support or applicable laws or regulations. All such invention disclosures so filed are attached hereto as Appendix ___ to this Agreement.

ARTICLE III - ROYALTIES, PAYMENTS

3.1   Licensee shall pay to University a non-refundable license fee in the amount of $_____ upon execution of this Agreement, and a further non-refundable fee of $_____ upon the issuance of the first Patent Right to be issued as a U.S. patent.

3.2   Licensee shall pay to University milestone fees as set forth below within thirty (30) days following the end of the calendar quarter in which the first Licensed Product of Licensee, Affiliate or Sublicensee achieves any of the following milestones:

[INSERT TABLE OF MILESTONE EVENTS AND FEES]

3.3   If Licensee or its Affiliates or Sublicensees makes and sells Licensed Products to End Users, then Licensee shall pay University during the License Term a royalty of _____ percent (____%) of the End User Net Sales of such Licensed Products.

3.4   If Licensee or its Affiliates or Sublicensees make and sell Licensed Products to Distributors, then Licensee shall pay University during the License Term a royalty of _____ percent (____%) of the Bulk Net Sales of such Licensed Products.

3.5   In addition, Licensee shall pay University a royalty equal to _____ percent (____%) of Fee Revenues received from the third party during the first year following the Effective Date, _____ percent (____%) of Fee Revenues received from the third party during the second year following the Effective Date, and _____ percent (___%) of Fee Revenues received from the third party thereafter during the License Term; provided, however, that if and to the extent that any such Fee Revenues are received due to the occurrence of a milestone that is described in Section 3.2, the amount payable to University under Section 3.2 with respect to such occurrence shall be credited against the amount payable under this Section 3.5 with respect to such receipt. Notwithstanding the foregoing, the royalty under this Section 3.5 with respect to Fee Revenues received under a sublicense, if any, entered by Licensee pursuant to Subclause 2.4(f)(ii)(B), except in circumstances in which Licensee had been engaged in discussions with the applicable sublicensee prior to the notice from University under Clause 2.4(f)(ii), shall be _____ percent (___%), rather than the percentage noted above in this Section 3.5.

3.6   Royalty payments on sales of Licensed Products by Licensee are payable and due by Licensee to the University within sixty (60) days after the end of each calendar quarter, during the License Term. Royalty payments on sales of Licensed Products by Licensee's Sublicensee(s) or Affiliates are payable and due to the University within sixty (60) days after the end of the calendar quarter in which Licensee receives payment from the Sublicensee or Affiliate. Milestone payments are payable and due by the Licensee to the University within thirty (30) days after the end of the calendar quarter in which the milestone was achieved. University's portion of other Fee Revenues received by Licensee is payable and due by the Licensee to the University within thirty (30) days after the end of the calendar quarter in which the Fee Revenues were received.

3.7   Beginning on the ____ anniversary of the Effective Date, Licensee shall also pay minimum annual fees as follows: $_____ on the _____, _____, _____, and _____ anniversary dates, and $_____ on each anniversary thereafter during the License Term. These minimum annual fees are reducible by other revenue paid by Licensee to University during the year, including all royalty, non-royalty income, and milestone payments.

ARTICLE IV - REPORTING

4.1   Licensee shall provide written annual reports within sixty (60) days after June 30 of each calendar year which shall include but not be limited to: reports of progress on research and development, regulatory approvals, manufacturing, sublicensing, marketing and sales during the preceding twelve (12) months as well as plans for the coming year. Licensee shall also provide any reasonable additional data University requires to evaluate Licensee's performance.

4.2   Licensee shall report to University the date of first commercial sale of Licensed Products (the "First Commercial Sale") in each country within thirty (30) days of occurrence.

4.3

(a) Licensee agrees, following the First Commercial Sale, to submit to University within thirty (30) days after the calendar quarters ending March 31, June 30, September 30, and December 31, reports setting forth for the preceding three (3) month period at least the following information:

(i) the number of the Licensed Products sold by Licensee, its Affiliates and Sublicensees in each country;
(ii) total billings for such Licensed Products;
(iii) deductions applicable to determine the Net Sales thereof, and the portions thereof that were Bulk Net Sales and End User Net Sales, respectively;
(iv) the amount of royalty due thereon;

and with each such royalty report to pay the amount of royalty due. Such report shall be certified as correct by an officer of Licensee and shall include a detailed listing of all deductions from royalties as specified herein. If no royalties are due to University for any reporting period, the written report shall so state.

(b) All payments due hereunder shall be payable in United States dollars. Conversion of foreign currency to U.S. dollars shall be made at the conversion rate existing in the United States (as reported in the Wall Street Journal) on the last working day of each royalty period. Such payments shall be without deduction of exchange, collection or other charges.

(c) All such reports shall be maintained in confidence by University, except as required by law, including Public Law 96-517 and 98-620.

(d) Late payments shall be subject to an interest charge of the lesser of one percent (1%) per month or the highest rate permitted by applicable law.

ARTICLE V - RECORD KEEPING

5.1 Licensee shall keep, and shall require its Affiliates and Sublicensees to keep, accurate and correct records of Licensed Products made, used or sold under this Agreement, appropriate to determine the amount of royalties due hereunder to University. Such records shall be retained for at least three (3) years following a given reporting period. They shall be available during normal business hours for inspection at the expense of University by a Certified Public Accountant selected by University and approved by Licensee for the sole purpose of verifying reports and payments hereunder. Such accountant shall not disclose to University any information other than information relating to accuracy of reports and payments made under this Agreement. In the event that any such inspection shows an underreporting and underpayment in excess of five percent (5%) for any twelve (12) month period in the aggregate as to all royalties payable to University hereunder during such period, then Licensee shall pay the reasonable cost of such examination (but not in excess of the amount of such underpayment) as well as any additional sum that would have been payable to University had the Licensee reported correctly, plus interest.

ARTICLE VI - FILING, PROSECUTION AND MAINTENANCE OF PATENTS

6.1 University shall take responsibility for the preparation, filing, prosecution and maintenance of any and all patent applications and patents included in Patent Rights. University shall engage patent counsel reasonably acceptable to Licensee for these purposes, which, with respect to US patent activities and to coordinating the work of foreign counsel, shall be the firm of _____, unless the Parties otherwise agree. University shall copy, and shall instruct patent counsel to copy, Licensee on all related prosecution correspondence promptly, and shall seek Licensee's counsel concerning all proposed courses of action materially affecting the Patent Rights. Upon request, University shall coordinate joint conferences to ensure that Licensee has adequate direct communication with patent counsel. University shall seek direction from Licensee on the geographic scope of patent protection it wishes to sponsor, and advise of and seek commentary on all proposed courses of action in any interference proceedings.

6.2   Within thirty (30) days after receiving University's invoice following the Effective Date, Licensee shall reimburse University for all reasonable expenses University has incurred for the preparation, filing, prosecution and maintenance of Patent Rights. As of invoices received through _____200__, patent expenses are: $_____. Licensee further agrees to reimburse University for all such reasonable future expenses within thirty (30) days after receipt of invoices from University; provided, however, that where University has granted any rights under the Patent Rights outside the Field, or has granted any Subfield-specific license pursuant to Subclause 2.4(f)(ii)(C), a reasonable allocation will be made of the portions of such expenses that are attributable specifically to the Field (which shall be reimbursed by Licensee) and otherwise (which will remain the responsibility of University or its other licensee). Late payment of these invoices shall be subject to interest charges of one percent (1%) per month.

6.3   University and Licensee shall cooperate fully in the preparation, filing, prosecution and maintenance of Patent Rights and of all patents and patent applications licensed to Licensee hereunder, executing all papers and instruments or requiring members of University to execute such papers and instruments as to enable University to apply for, to prosecute and to maintain patent applications and patents in University's name in any country. Each Party shall provide to the other prompt notice as to all matters which come to its attention and which may affect the preparation, filing, prosecution or maintenance of any such patent applications or patents.

6.4   If Licensee elects to no longer pay the reasonable expenses of a patent application or patent included within Patent Rights, Licensee shall notify University not less than sixty (60) days prior to such action and shall thereby surrender its rights under such patent or patent application.

ARTICLE VII - MARKING

7.1 If a patent under the Patent Rights has been or is subsequently issued to University covering any feature or features of the Licensed Products, Licensee agrees to mark each package or container in which the Licensed Products are sold by or for Licensee with marking complying with the provisions of United States law relating to the marking of patented devices, or with marking complying with the law of the country where the Licensed Products are shipped, used or sold.

ARTICLE VIII - INFRINGEMENT

8.1 With respect to any Patent Rights under which Licensee is exclusively licensed pursuant to this Agreement, Licensee or its Affiliate or Sublicensee shall have the right to prosecute in its own name and at its own expense any infringement of such patent, so long as such license is exclusive at the time of the commencement of such action within the scope or field applicable to such action. University agrees to notify Licensee promptly of each infringement of such patents of which University is or becomes aware. Before Licensee or its Affiliate or Sublicensee commences an action with respect to any infringement of such patents Licensee shall give careful consideration to the views of University and to potential effects on the public interest in making its decision whether or not to sue and Licensee shall report such views to its Affiliate or Sublicensee where applicable.

8.2 If Licensee elects to sue for patent infringement, University agrees to be named as nominal third party plaintiff if necessary to the commencement of any such action, and further agrees to provide any information available to University and needed by Licensee in prosecuting such action. Licensee shall reimburse University for any costs it incurs as part of an action brought by Licensee or its Sublicensee, irrespective of whether University shall become a co-plaintiff.

8.3   If Licensee or its Sublicensee elects to commence an action as described above, Licensee may reduce, by up to fifty percent (50%), the royalty due to University earned under the patent subject to suit by fifty percent (50%) of the amount of the expenses and costs of such action, including attorney fees. In the event that such fifty percent (50%) of such expenses and costs exceed the amount of royalties withheld by Licensee for any calendar year, Licensee may to that extent reduce the royalties due to University from Licensee in succeeding calendar years, but never by more than fifty percent (50%) of the royalty due in any one year.

8.4   No settlement, consent judgment or other voluntary final disposition of the suit may be entered into without the consent of University, which consent shall not be unreasonably withheld.

8.5   Recoveries or reimbursements from such action shall first be applied to reimburse Licensee and University for litigation costs not paid from royalties and then to reimburse University for royalties withheld. Any remaining recoveries or reimbursements shall be treated as Fee Revenues covered by Section 3.5.

8.6   In the event that Licensee and its Sublicensee, if any, elect not to exercise their right to prosecute an infringement of the Patent Rights pursuant to the above sections, University may do so at its own expense, controlling such action and retaining all recoveries therefrom.

8.7   If a claim or action seeking a declaratory judgment that any of the Patent Rights is invalid shall be made or brought against Licensee and/or University, then each of Licensee and University shall have the right to intervene in and to participate in the defense of such claim or action at its own expense.

8.8   University shall have no obligation to defend any action for infringement brought against Licensee by a third party. In the event Licensee is sued by a third party, and as a result of the settlement of such suit required to pay a royalty to a third party on a Licensed Product or a Licensed Process, the amount of royalty paid will be deducted from the royalty payment due to the University for that Licensed Product. In the event the settlement prevents the Licensee from continuing sales of a

Licensed Product, no additional royalties will apply for that Licensed Product and the minimum fees under Section 3.7 will thereupon be abated in their entirety.

ARTICLE IX - TERMINATION OF AGREEMENT

9.1   Upon any termination of this Agreement, and except as provided herein to the contrary, all rights and obligations of the Parties hereunder shall cease, except as follows:

   (a) University's right to receive or recover and Licensee's obligation to pay royalties accrued for payment at the time of any termination;
   (b) Licensee's obligation to maintain records and University's right to conduct a final audit as provided in Article V of this Agreement; and
   (c) Any cause of action or claim of University, accrued because of any breach or default by Licensee.

9.2   In the event Licensee fails to make payments due hereunder, University shall have the right to terminate this Agreement upon forty-five (45) days written notice, unless Licensee makes such payments plus interest within the forty-five (45) day notice period; provided, however, that if there is a good faith dispute as to the amount purported to be due and payable, such 45-day period will not start to run until such dispute has been resolved. Both Parties agree to use commercially reasonable efforts to resolve any dispute arising under this Section 9.2 between themselves using due and deliberate speed.

9.3   In the event that Licensee shall be in default in the performance of any obligations under this Agreement (other than as provided in Section 9.2 above which shall take precedence over any other default), and if the default has not been remedied within ninety (90) days after the date of notice in writing of such default, University may terminate this Agreement immediately by written notice; provided, however, that if there is a good faith dispute as to the existence of such default, such 90-day period will not start to run until such dispute has been resolved. Both Parties agree to use commercially reasonable efforts to resolve any dispute arising under this Section 9.3 between themselves using due and deliberate speed.

9.4   In the event that Licensee shall become insolvent, shall make an assignment for the benefit of creditors, or shall have a petition in bankruptcy filed for or against it, University shall have the right to terminate this entire Agreement immediately upon giving Licensee written notice of such termination.

9.5   Any sublicenses granted by Licensee under this Agreement shall provide for termination or assignment to University, at the option of University, of Licensee's interest therein, to the extent accruing after such assignment, to be effective upon termination of this Agreement.

9.6   Licensee shall have the right to terminate this Agreement in whole or in part with respect to any Licensed Product or any Subfield by giving ninety (90) days advance written notice to University. Upon termination, a final report shall be submitted and any royalty payments and unreimbursed patent expenses due to University become immediately payable.

9.7   Licensee shall have the right during a period of six (6) months following the effective date of such termination to sell or otherwise dispose of the Licensed Product existing at the time of such termination, and shall make a final report and payment of all royalties related thereto within sixty (60) days following the end of such period or the date of the final disposition of such inventory, whichever first occurs.

9.8   Any partial termination of this Agreement with respect to any Licensed Product or any Subfield shall not alter the rights and obligations of the Parties as to the remaining aspects of this Agreement. Further, termination of this Agreement shall not obviate the rights and obligations accrued by each Party prior to termination.

ARTICLE X - REPRESENTATIONS AND WARRANTIES: LIMITATIONS

10.1   Nothing in this Agreement shall be construed as:

    (a) A warranty or representation by University as to the validity or scope of any of the Patent Rights; or

(b) Conferring a right to use in advertising, publicity or otherwise the name of the University, or the inventors, unless University has specifically approved the same in writing.

10.2   University represents and warrants that: (i) it has not granted any previous right or license under any of the Patent Rights, whether within or outside the Field; (ii) it will not grant any right or license during the License Term inconsistent with the rights and licenses granted to Licensee hereunder; (iii) to the best of its knowledge as of the Effective Date, anything made, used or sold under this Agreement will be free from infringement of patents of third parties; and (iv) University has no received any notice or claim, nor is it party to or subject to any suit or proceeding (including without limitation patent interferences), claiming that any of the Patent Rights are invalid or unpatentable, or that any Licensed Products or Licensed Processes would infringe upon or misappropriate the intellectual properties or other rights of any third party.

10.3   OTHERWISE, UNIVERSITY EXPRESSLY DISCLAIMS ANY AND ALL IMPLIED OR EXPRESS WARRANTIES AND MAKES NO EXPRESS OR IMPLIED WARRANTIES OF MERCHANTABILITY OR FITNESS FOR ANY PARTICULAR PURPOSE OF THE PATENT RIGHTS OR INFORMATION SUPPLIED BY UNIVERSITY, LICENSED PROCESSES OR LICENSED PRODUCTS CONTEMPLATED BY THIS AGREEMENT. University assumes no responsibilities whatever with respect to design, development, manufacture, use, sale or other disposition by Licensee or Affiliates of Licensed Products or Licensed Processes. The entire risk as to the design, development, manufacture, offering for sale, sale, or other disposition and performance of Licensed Products and Licensed Processes is assumed by Licensee and Affiliates.

ARTICLE XI – INDEMNITY AND INSURANCE

11.1   Licensee shall indemnify, defend and hold harmless University and its current or former directors, governing board members, trustees, officers, faculty, medical and professional staff, employees, students, and agents and their respective successors, heirs and assigns (the "Indemnitees"), against any liability, damage, loss or expenses (including reasonable attorneys' fees and expenses of litigation) incurred by or imposed upon the Indemnitees or any one of them in connection with any third party claims, suits, actions, demands or judgments arising out any theory of product liability (including, but not limited to, actions in the form of tort, warranty, or strict liability) concerning any product, process or service made, used or sold pursuant to any right or license granted under this Agreement, provided that the Indemnitee promptly notifies Licensee of any such claim, suit, action or demand, tenders control of the defense and settlement thereof to Licensee, and reasonably cooperates as requested in such defense. Notwithstanding the foregoing, Licensee shall not be required to indemnify any Indemnitee to the extent that any liability, damage, loss or expenses are the result of any Indemnitee's gross negligence or willful misconduct.

11.2   Licensee agrees, at its own expense, to provide attorneys reasonably acceptable to University to defend against any actions brought or filed against any Indemnitee with respect to the subject of indemnity contained herein, whether or not such actions are rightfully brought.

11.3   Beginning at the time as any such product, process or service is being commercially distributed or sold (other than for the purpose of obtaining regulatory approvals) by Licensee or by a Sublicensee, Affiliate or agent of Licensee, Licensee shall, at its sole cost and expense procure and maintain commercial general liability insurance in amounts not less than $_____$ per incident and $_____$ annual aggregate and naming the University as an additional insured. During clinical trials of any such product, process or service Licensee shall, at its sole cost and expense, procure and maintain commercial general liability insurance in such equal or lesser amounts as University shall reasonably require, naming the University as additional insureds. Such commercial general liability insurance shall provide (i) product liability coverage and (ii) broad form contractual liability coverage for Licensee's indemnification under this Agreement. If Licensee elects to self-insure all or part of the limits described above (including deductibles or retentions which are in excess of $_____ annual aggregate) such self-insurance program must be approved by University, which approval shall not be unreasonably withheld. The minimum amounts of insurance coverage required shall not be construed to create a limit of Licensee's liability with respect to its indemnification under this Agreement.

11.4   Licensee shall provide University with written evidence of such insurance upon request of University. Licensee shall provide University with written notice at least fifteen (15) days prior to the cancellation, non-renewal or material change in such insurance; if Licensee does not obtain replacement insurance providing comparable coverage within such fifteen (15) day period, University shall have the right to suspend Licensee's rights and licenses (but not its obligations) under this Agreement effective at the end of such fifteen (15) day period, and, if Licensee has not obtained such replacement insurance within a further ninety (90) days, University shall thereafter have the right to terminate this Agreement by notice to Licensee, if such notice is given prior Licensee's obtaining such replacement insurance.

11.5   Licensee shall maintain such commercial general liability insurance beyond the expiration or termination of this Agreement during (i) the period that any product, process, or service, relating to, or developed pursuant to, this Agreement is being commercially distributed or sold by Licensee or by a Sublicensee, Affiliate or agent of Licensee and (ii) a reasonable period after the period referred to in (e)(i) above which in no event shall be less than six (6) years.

ARTICLE XII – OTHER AGREEMENTS

12.1   Licensee shall exert reasonable efforts to consider the eligibility of the University to participate in Licensee's clinical trials of Licensed Products. Where The University is so eligible and is at least as appropriate a venue for such trials as other candidates, Licensee and University shall attempt in good faith to enter a commercially and clinically satisfactory agreement governing the conduct of such clinical trials at the University. Any such agreement will be subject to review and approval by the University and Licensee to assure that any such trials are conducted according to all applicable laws and regulations and the internal procedures of each Party.

12.2   The University and Licensee agree to enter good faith negotiations for the conduct of further research at the University on the Patent Rights and related technology. Such negotiations and outcome of such negotiations shall not affect any of the terms agreed to by the Parties as set forth in this License Agreement.

ARTICLE XIII – DISPUTE RESOLUTION

13.1   In the event of any controversy or claim arising out of or relating to any provision of this Agreement or the breach thereof, the Parties shall try to settle such conflicts amicably between themselves. Any such conflict which the Parties are unable to resolve, other than matters relating to patent validity, shall be settled through arbitration conducted in accordance with the rules of the American Arbitration Association. In the event a dispute is arbitrated, the demand for arbitration shall be filed within a reasonable time after the controversy or claim has arisen, and in no event after the date upon which institution of legal proceedings based on such controversy or claim would be barred by the applicable statutes of limitation. Such arbitration shall be held in _____. The award through arbitration shall be final and binding. Either Party may enter any such award in a court having jurisdiction or may make application to such court for judicial acceptance of the award and an order of enforcement, as the case may be. The cost of the arbitration shall be split equally between the Parties, unless the arbitrator determines that a Party has incurred unreasonable expenses due to vexatious or bad faith positions taken by the other Party, in which event the arbitrator may make an award of all or any portion of such expenses so incurred. Notwithstanding the foregoing, either party may, without recourse to arbitration, assert against the other Party a third party claim or cross claim in any action brought by a third party, to which the subject matter of this Agreement may be relevant. Notwithstanding the foregoing, either Party may seek a preliminary injunction or other interim judicial relief at any time if in its judgment such action is necessary to avoid irreparable damage.

ARTICLE XIV - GENERAL

14.1   The rights and licenses granted by University in this Agreement are specific and may not be assigned or otherwise transferred to any third party, other than an Affiliate, without the prior written approval of University, except that no such approval will be required where the assignment or transfer is made in connection with the transfer of all or substantially all the assets of the business of Licensee or Affiliate relating to the applicable Patent Rights. Any attempted assignment or transfer without any such required approval shall be void.

14.2   The Parties intend that this Agreement will be construed and enforced to be consistent with all applicable laws, and they do not intend to violate hereby any public policy or statutory or common law. To the extent any provision of this Agreement is invalid, illegal, or unenforceable, such provision shall be enforced to the maximum extent permitted by law and the Parties' fundamental intentions hereunder, and the remaining provisions shall not be affected or impaired.

14.3   No waiver by a Party of any breach of this Agreement, no matter how long continuing or how often repeated, shall be deemed a waiver of any subsequent breach thereof, nor shall any delay or omission on the part of a Party to exercise any right, power or privilege hereunder be deemed a waiver of such right, power or privilege.

14.4   The relationship between the Parties is that of independent contractors. Licensee shall not be deemed to be an agent of University in connection with the exercise of any rights hereunder, and shall not have any right or authority to assume or create any obligation or responsibility on behalf of University.

14.5   No Party hereto shall be deemed to be in default of any provision of this Agreement, or for any failure in performance, resulting from acts or events beyond the reasonable control of such Party, such as acts of God, acts of civil or military authority, civil disturbance, terrorism, war, strikes, fires, power failures, natural catastrophes or other "force majeure" events whether similar or dissimilar to the foregoing.

14.6   Any notice, report or payment provided for in this Agreement shall be given if in writing and shall be effective on the earlier of actual receipt or the third day after being sent by express courier or certified or registered mail addressed to the Party for whom intended at the address set forth below, or to such address as either Party may hereafter designate in writing to the other:

(a) For the University:

(b) For the Licensee:

14.7   This Agreement shall be construed, interpreted, and applied in accordance with the laws of the State of _____.

14.8   Licensee agrees to comply with all applicable laws and regulations. In particular, it is understood and acknowledged that the transfer of certain commodities and technical data is subject to United States laws and regulations controlling the export of such commodities and technical data, including all Export Administration Regulations of the United States Department of Commerce. These laws and regulations among other things, prohibit or require a license for the export of certain types of technical data to certain specified countries. Licensee hereby agrees and gives written assurance that it will comply with all United States laws and regulations controlling the export of commodities and technical data, that it will be solely responsible for any violation of such by Licensee or its Affiliates or sublicensees, and that it will defend and hold University harmless in the event of any legal action of any nature occasioned by such violation.

14.9   This Agreement constitutes the final and entire agreement between the Parties, and supersedes all prior written agreements and any prior or contemporaneous oral understanding regarding the subject matter hereof. Any representation, promise or condition in connection with such subject matter which is not incorporated in this Agreement shall not be binding on either Party. No modification, renewal, extension or termination of this Agreement or any of its provisions shall be binding upon the Party against whom enforcement of such modification, renewal, extension or termination is sought, unless made in writing and signed on behalf of such Party by a duly authorized officer.

[Signature page follows]

IN WITNESS WHEREOF, each of the Parties have caused this Agreement to be executed in one or more counterparts by its duly authorized representative, to be effective as of the Effective Date.

UNIVERSITY

By: _____

Name: _____

Title: _____

Date Signed: _____

LICENSEE

By: _____

Name: _____

Title: _____

Date Signed: _____

Courtesy of Daniel Yost, Lou Soto, and Mitch Zuklie, Orrick, Herrington and Sutcliffe LLP

APPENDIX C

AGREEMENT TO RELEASE INTERSTATE PIPELINE CAPACITY AND FIRM TRANSPORTATION CONTRACT RIGHTS

THIS AGREEMENT FOR THE RELEASE OF INTERSTATE PIPELINE CAPACITY AND ASSOCIATED FIRM TRANSPORTATION CONTRACT RIGHTS ("this Agreement" or the "Release Agreement") is made and entered into as of the 18th day of April, 200_ by and between _____ Corporation ("SELLER" or the "Releasing Shipper"), and _____ Company ("BUYER" or the "Replacement Shipper"). Capitalized terms not defined herein shall have the meaning set forth in the Tariff.

WHEREAS, SELLER is the holder of at least _____ dekatherms ("Dth") per day of firm transportation service on the interstate pipeline owned by _____Pipeline ("PIPELINE") in Pipeline's Rate Zone__ and has the ability to release and transfer some or all of its contract and firm capacity rights on a temporary or permanent basis under rules and regulations of the Federal Energy Regulatory Commission ("FERC") and PIPELINE's FERC Gas Tariff (the "Tariff");

WHEREAS, SELLER' firm transportation contract with PIPELINE is in the "evergreen period" pursuant to which either party must give _____ years' prior notice of its intent to terminate the contract;

WHEREAS, SELLER is willing to release and transfer _____ Dth per day of its firm capacity and related firm transportation contract rights on PIPELINE to BUYER as a temporary release under the Tariff for five successive one-year terms beginning May 1, 200_ under the terms and conditions set forth in this Agreement;

WHEREAS, BUYER desires to accept the release of _____ Dth per day of firm capacity from SELLER under the terms and conditions set forth in this Agreement and to execute a firm transportation service agreement with PIPELINE as a Replacement Shipper under the Tariff;

NOW, THEREFORE, in consideration of the premises and the mutual covenants herein contained, SELLER and BUYER do hereby agree as follows

I. RELEASE QUANTITY

SELLER hereby agrees to release and transfer to BUYER, and BUYER agrees to accept and to enter into a replacement shipper contract with PIPELINE for the foregoing firm transportation quantity of _____ Dth per day in PIPELINE's Rate Zone __ (the "Released Capacity").

II. CHARACTERISTICS OF THE RELEASE

A. <u>Receipt and Delivery Points</u>. The release shall be an intrazone release in PIPELINE's Rate Zone __.

    1. Receipt Point. The Receipt Point for the Released Capacity shall be at Milepost _____.

    2. Delivery Point: The Delivery Points for the Released Capacity shall be at Milepost _____.

B. <u>Term</u>. Provided that BUYER is not in default of its obligations under this Agreement, the release shall be five (5) successive terms of one year each, beginning on the Gas Day (as defined in the Tariff) on May 1st and ending at the close of the Gas Day on April 30th (the "Contract Year"). The first Contract Year shall begin at the start of the Gas Day on May 1, 200_ and end at the close of the Gas Day on April 30, 200_.

C. <u>SELLER' Recall Rights</u>. SELLER shall have the right to recall the Released Capacity pursuant to the Tariff as follows:

    1. <u>Default</u>. Immediately in the event of a default by BUYER under this Agreement; provided, however, that SELLER shall give written notice to BUYER prior to or concurrently with the exercise of such recall and shall comply with any notice provisions in the Tariff;

2. **Five and Ten Day Recall Option.** During each Contract Year, SELLER shall have the option ("recall option") to recall the Released Capacity for any five (5) or ten (10) days (each such day a "recall day") during the five-month period from the beginning of the November 1st Gas Day through the end of the March 31st Gas Day (the "Winter Period"). The recall days may be consecutive or nonconsecutive at SELLER's election. The Released Capacity shall be reput and revert to BUYER after the close of the recall day(s). SELLER shall notify BUYER in writing of SELLER's decision with respect to the recall option for the Winter Period of each Contract Year not later than September 1 of the then current Contract Year.

3. **Prior Notice of Daily Recall.** During any Contract Year in which SELLER exercises the five-day or ten-day recall option, SELLER shall notify BUYER of its election to recall the Released Capacity for a Gas Day not later than 8:00 AM Central Clock Time on the day prior to the Gas Day of the recall. Unless BUYER and SELLER mutually agree to the contrary, SELLER shall be required to recall the Released Capacity for the number of days specified in the notice in which the option is exercised.

D. **Rates for the Released Capacity.** This is a "Reservation Rate" release of the Released Capacity pursuant to the terms of the Tariff. BUYER shall pay the effective maximum monthly reservation rate per Dth of Released Capacity for firm transportation service under PIPELINE's Rate Schedule FT for Zone ___ to Zone ___ transportation, including any and all reservation surcharges applicable under the Tariff, and all volumetric charges and surcharges applicable to such transportation, as such reservation and volumetric rates and charges may be changed from time to time by PIPELINE during the term of this Agreement.

E. **Rates for Recalled Capacity under the Options.** If SELLER exercises either the five-day or ten-day recall option in any Contract Year, then, on each day the Released Capacity is recalled, SELLER shall pay to PIPELINE the applicable maximum daily reservation rate for the Released Capacity (including any reservation surcharges).

III. COMPLIANCE WITH THE TARIFF AND FERC RULES AND REGULATIONS

A. *Compliance with the Tariff and FERC Rules*. This Agreement and the release of the Released Capacity hereunder are subject to the rules and regulations of the Federal Energy Regulatory Commission and the terms and conditions of the Tariff.

B. *The Release Request*. Prior to each Contract Year, SELLER shall submit the release to PIPELINE as a non-biddable, pre-arranged maximum rate release sufficiently in advance of the start of the Contract Year for PIPELINE to award the capacity and contract rights to BUYER and shall include the recall and reput conditions and rates for the Released Capacity agreed to herein. If PIPELINE or the FERC changes its rules or otherwise determines that the release must be subject to bidding, then SELLER shall make the release available for bids for the minimum period of time required under the Tariff or applicable FERC rules.

C. *Award of the Released Capacity*. BUYER shall promptly enter into a service agreement with PIPELINE for the Released Capacity after the award from PIPELINE. Notwithstanding this Agreement, if BUYER elects to accept different terms by exercising its right to match the terms offered by another bidder under any bidding process required by PIPELINE or FERC for the Released Capacity, then the terms accepted by BUYER shall supercede and replace the applicable terms in this Agreement.

IV. RECALL OPTION FEE

On September 1 of any Contract Year in which SELLER elects to purchase from BUYER one of the recall options set forth in Section II.C.2 of this Agreement, SELLER shall pay to BUYER the following fee as consideration for BUYER's offering the option, which payment shall be made not later than September 30 of the Contract Year, or, if September 30 falls on a Saturday, Sunday or holiday, the next business day thereafter:

A. Five-Day Recall Option: If SELLER elects the five-day recall option, the fee shall be _____ _____

B. Ten-Day Recall Option: If SELLER elects the ten-day recall option, the fee shall be _____

V. TERM CONTINGENCY

SELLER shall not exercise its right to cancel its FT Service Agreement with PIPELINE for the Released Capacity pursuant to the evergreen provision of said FT Service Agreement in a manner that would prevent SELLER from releasing the Released Capacity to BUYER. SELLER shall promptly notify BUYER if PIPELINE gives SELLER notice of cancellation of the FT Service Agreement that includes the Released Capacity, and the cancellation or termination of said FT Service Agreement by PIPELINE would make the Released Capacity unavailable for release by SELLER to BUYER. SELLER shall not be obligated to release the Released Capacity to BUYER and should not be liable to BUYER for SELLER's inability to release the Released Capacity during a Contract Year if the termination or cancellation by PIPELINE of the FT Service Agreement for the Released Capacity has become effective.

VI. DEFAULT

A. Events of Default. Events of default under this Agreement are as follows: Either party (the "Defaulting Party") (i) makes an assignment or any general arrangement for the benefit of creditors; (ii) files a petition or otherwise commence, authorize, or acquiesce in the commencement of a proceeding or case under any bankruptcy or similar law for the protection of creditors or has such petition filed or proceeding commenced against it; (iii) otherwise becomes bankrupt or insolvent (reasonably evidenced); (iv) is unable to pay its debts as they fall due; (v) has a receiver, provisional liquidator, conservator, custodian, trustee or other similar official appointed with respect to it or substantially all of its assets; (vi) has its credit rating and/or the credit rating of its long-term senior debt reduced to below investment grade by any one or more of the rating services (currently Moody's, Standard & Poor and Fitch), and said party fails to provide adequate assurance of its ability to perform its obligations hereunder, including the guarantee of a creditworthy third party within two (2) Business Days of a written request by the other party; or (vii) not have paid any amount due to PIPELINE with respect to the Released Capacity on or before the second Business Day following written Notice that such payment is overdue.

B. <u>Remedies</u>. If an Event of Default occurs with respect to either Party at any time during the term of this Agreement, the other Party shall have the right, at its sole election, to establish a date on which this Agreement shall terminate and/or, where applicable, recall the Released Capacity as provided for in Section II.C.1 of this Agreement. In the event of such termination the non-defaulting Party shall be entitled to any remedies available at law or under this Agreement, including without limitation the right to cover damages.

VII. MISCELLANEOUS

A. <u>Notices</u>. All notices hereunder, except those specifically provided for under other provisions hereof, shall be deemed duly given if in writing and sent by postpaid registered or certified mail addressed to the respective Parties at the addresses stated below or such other addresses as they shall respectively hereafter designate in writing from time to time, except dispatching notices which may be given by telephone:

BUYER: <u>ALL NOTICES</u>

SELLER: <u>ALL NOTICES</u>

B. <u>Waivers</u>. A waiver by either Party of any one or more defaults by the other in the performance of any provisions of this Agreement will not operate as a waiver of any future default or defaults, whether of a like or of a different character.

C. <u>Entire Agreement</u>. This Agreement, the attachments and exhibits hereto, constitute the entire agreement between the Parties relating to the subject matter contemplated by this Agreement. There are no prior or contemporaneous agreements or representations (whether oral or written) affecting the subject matter other than those herein expressed. No amendment or modification to this Agreement shall be enforceable, unless reduced in writing and executed by both Parties. The provisions of this Agreement shall not impart rights enforceable by any person, firm or organization not a Party or not bound as a Party, or not a permitted successor or assignee of a Party bound to this Agreement.

D. <u>Limitation of Damages</u>. FOR BREACH OF ANY PROVISION FOR WHICH AN EXPRESS REMEDY OR MEASURE OF DAMAGES IS HEREIN PROVIDED, SUCH EXPRESS REMEDY OR MEASURE OF DAMAGES SHALL BE THE SOLE AND EXCLUSIVE REMEDY HEREUNDER, THE OBLIGOR'S LIABILITY SHALL BE LIMITED AS SET FORTH IN SUCH PROVISION AND ALL OTHER REMEDIES OR DAMAGES AT LAW OR IN EQUITY ARE WAIVED. IF NO REMEDY OR MEASURE OF DAMAGES IS EXPRESSLY HEREIN PROVIDED, THE OBLIGOR'S LIABILITY SHALL BE LIMITED TO DIRECT ACTUAL DAMAGES ONLY, SUCH DIRECT ACTUAL DAMAGES SHALL BE THE SOLE AND EXCLUSIVE REMEDY HEREUNDER AND ALL OTHER REMEDIES OR DAMAGES AT LAW OR IN EQUITY ARE WAIVED. UNLESS EXPRESSLY HEREIN PROVIDED, NEITHER PARTY SHALL BE LIABLE FOR CONSEQUENTIAL, INCIDENTAL, PUNITIVE, EXEMPLARY OR INDIRECT DAMAGES, LOST PROFITS, OR OTHER BUSINESS INTERRUPTION DAMAGES, IN TORT, CONTRACT, UNDER ANY INDEMNITY PROVISION OR OTHERWISE.

E. **No Implied Warranties**. EXCEPT FOR WARRANTING THAT SELLER HAS OR WILL HAVE GOOD TITLE TO THE RELEASED CAPACITY UNLESS THE TERM CONTINGENCY IN ARTICLE V OCCURS, SELLER MAKES AND BUYER RECEIVES NO OTHER WARRANTIES, EXPRESS OR IMPLIED, AND THERE ARE EXPRESSLY EXCLUDED ALL WARRANTIES OF MERCHANTABILITY AND FITNESS FOR A PARTICULAR PURPOSE.

F. **Choice of Law**. This Agreement shall be construed and interpreted in accordance with the laws of the State of _____, except for the laws of the State of _____ pertaining to choice of law.

G. **Authority**. Each Party represents and warrants that it has the authority to enter into this agreement, and any person signing this Agreement on the Party's behalf does so with the authority of the Party.

H. **Counterparts**. This Agreement may be executed in one or more counterparts, each of which shall be deemed an original and all of which shall be taken together and deemed to be one instrument.

[SIGNATURES ON FOLLOWING PAGE]

IN TESTIMONY WHEREOF, the Parties hereto have caused this Agreement to be duly signed and sealed, the day and year first above written.

SELLER

BUYER

By: _____

By: _____

Title: _____

Title: _____

Courtesy of Jeffrey D. Komarow, Bradley Arant Rose & White LLP

ASPATORE BOOKS